BASIC BIBLE SERIES

FIRST AND SECOND THESSALONIANS

HOPE OF HIS COMING

BASIC BIBLE SERIES

FIRST AND SECOND THESSALONIANS

HOPE OF HIS COMING

DAVID C. COOK PUBLISHING CO.
ELGIN, IL 60120

This Basic Bible Series study was developed through the combined efforts and resources of a number of David C. Cook's dedicated lesson writers. It was compiled and edited by John Sheetz, designed by Melanie Lawson and Dawn Lauck, with cover art by Richard Sparks.
—Gary Wilde, Series Editor

I and II Thessalonians: Hope of His Coming

ISBN: 0-89191-520-6
Library of Congress Catalog Number: 86-70884

I Thessalonians 1:3

Inspired by hope in
our Lord Jesus Christ.

Contents

1

A Church's Witness

Truth to Apply: My church's witness is measured by the example it has become to all who know its members.

Key Verse: We continually remember before our God and Father your work produced by faith, your labor prompted by love, and your endurance inspired by hope in our Lord Jesus Christ (I Thess. 1:3).

"One of life's humbling and heartwarming experiences is to reflect on the best things that have happened to us—to know why few of them have come by our own efforts, and how many can be credited to someone else's gentle, persuasive influence. Another's prayers overheard; a church school teacher's lessons presented humbly; a minister's quiet insight and wisdom when we are bewildered; the silent handclasp of a friend whose heart is too full to permit words; a child's dependence upon us for strength and example; a card in the mail; a phone call. Such influences are God's instruments. . . . The Gospel has an unobtrusive, but quietly powerful, effect upon others. While living today . . . we, too, have an unconscious influence. The witness of one Christ-filled life flavors a whole community" (A. G. Downing, *Crusader*).

In what ways, in your past experience, have you felt the witness of a church simply through the loving actions of an individual member? Is this a common experience? Why?

Introducing Thessalonians

The Thessalonian letters have been designated as Paul's eschatological epistles (eschatology is the study of "last things," that is, the Second Coming of Christ and all that attends it). Each chapter in I Thessalonians concludes with a reference to Christ's return.

Paul related the Second Coming to Christ's resurrection. The latter is the prelude to the former (Acts 17:31). Christ's followers rest their faith on these events as well as the virgin birth, the cross, and the ascension.

Why is this book important? Like all inspired Scripture, it reveals God's will to us, and thus gives us direction in our daily lives. Furthermore, it is important for four special reasons: its insights concerning the cultural climate of an ancient city, its early date, its doctrinal teaching, and its unique content.

Economic, Cultural, Religious Climate

What sort of place was Thessalonica? The city was a hub of commerce because it had a good harbor and was a main stop on the Roman military road connecting Dyrrhachium and Byzantium. Politically it was the seat of the Roman governor of Macedonia, but it was also a "free city." This meant the citizens could handle their own internal affairs. Thus we see the point of the political charge brought against Paul by the Jews (Acts 17:6-7).

Culturally, the city was largely Greek, but it was also a cosmopolitan center. People from East and West met there because of the commercial advantages and the political necessity to travel to Rome.

The world of the New Testament writhed in religious uncertainty. People were thinking for themselves, but were fearful of losing their souls in the process. Illustrative of the religious quandary was the attempt of Marcus Varro, in 47 B.C., to divide the ancient gods into three groups: "certain," or mythical gods, "uncertain," or rational gods (the philosophers' theories), and "select" gods (the civil religion).

Seneca, resident intellectual in the court of Nero during Paul's first imprisonment, illustrates well the religious climate of the day: "Go to the Capitol and what do you see? It is shameful to speak of the extravagance which the popular dementia has thought up, and performs as if a duty. One man is calling off names to Jupiter (as if announcing new arrivals!); another is telling him the time; one is washing him, while another is anointing him with oil."

Early Date

The early date of this letter (48-51 A.D.) lets us see the beginnings of the church in the West. Paul's first missionary journey had been limited to Asia Minor, but at Troas Paul dreamed a dream. A man from Macedonia called to him for help (Acts 16:6-10). Paul went, and God blessed his ministry at Philippi. Great ministries always bring opposition, and consequently Paul moved on to Thessalonica, where the same pattern was repeated. Both Jews and Greeks were converted. Persecution came and the missionaries moved on to Athens, but they were forced out before a church was firmly established. Naturally, Paul was concerned about those who were left without strong leadership, so he immediately wrote to these new converts. Thus, the letter was written only twenty years after the crucifixion, between 48 and 51 A.D., even before the Gospels.

Doctrinal Themes

Paul was very much concerned with teaching in this letter. These major doctrines are mentioned:

The Trinity (1:1; 1:5, 6).

The Holy Spirit (1:5, 6; 4:8; 5:19).

The Second Coming of Christ (1:10; 2:19; 3:13; 4:14-17; 5:23).

Assurance (1:5).

Conversion (1:9).

Election (1:4).

The Resurrection (4:14-18).

Sanctification (4:3; 5:23).

Apparently, those who argue that doctrine is unimportant to evangelism are proven wrong. What they rightly object to is *ineffective* doctrinal teaching. To communicate theological truth properly one must teach it like Paul, with an eye on how it applies to everyday life.

Unique Content

The fourth reason for a thorough study of these letters is their unique revelations. In one sense, of course, all Scripture is unique, but many passages have special emphasis. I John, for example, is the letter most concerned with love. To most people's minds the Thessalonian letters focus on eschatology, on what will happen in the future. Indeed, this is one major theme. However, these letters also focus on Christian sociology, that is, how the Gospel works in groups of people. Finally, they are a model, showing evangelism at work in a sophisticated environment—showing us how we can reach those in our own sophisticated environments.

Background/Overview: *I Thessalonians 1:1-5*

This chapter begins with a salutation (vs. 1) followed with a prayer of thanksgiving for the Thessalonians' positive response to the Gospel.

In the next section, Paul will express his confidence in their election. This confidence is based on their response to the missionary party, and their witness to others.

Light on the Text

1:1 "Paul, Silas and Timothy." "Silvanus" (KJV) is the Latin form of the Aramaic "Silas" (as he is always called in Acts).

Timothy was a young man who joined Paul at Lystra on his second missionary journey (Acts 16:1-4). He is mentioned in the salutations of no less than six of Paul's epistles. With the possible exception of Luke, their association was longer and more continuous than that of any of Paul's companions.

"The church of the Thessalonians." The word Paul uses for church, *ekklesia*, is derived from two Greek words: *ek,* meaning "out of," and *kaleo,* meaning "to call." It refers to those who are called out of a group for some purpose. In the pagan society it meant those who were summoned to a lawful assembly because they were citizens who could vote.

There are four New Testament uses of *ekklesia:* 1) All believers in Heaven and earth; 2) all Christians in a given area, as in Acts 9:31, "Then the church throughout Judea, Galilee and Samaria enjoyed a time of peace"; 3) all the Christians in a given city; 4) all the Christians in one's house. In all cases, the notion behind the word is that of a select group called together for some purpose. Christians are chosen by God and called by the Spirit for the purpose of establishing a ministry.

Here Paul is referring to those individuals who were called out of the pagan world of Thessalonica for identification with Christ. This idea of election appears later in verse 4 of this chapter.

"Grace." Grace is a distinctly Pauline opening, based on *chairein* ("rejoice"), the ordinary street greeting Greek people exchanged. It is a theological term describing the unmerited favor by which God gives us what we could never earn on our own. Our salvation is on the basis of Christ's death for our redemption—pure grace.

"Peace." By joining peace (the ordinary Jewish street greeting) to grace Paul captured the best of both worlds. To a Jew, peace included one's total welfare, a sense of wholeness (a concept modern psychologists might see as personal and social integration).

1:2, 3 In his prayer Paul remembers three parallel features (1:3), each of which has an outward, more measurable form (work, labor, and patience) and an inward, inspiring quality (the familiar Pauline triad of faith, love, and hope). Among other places where Paul's classic trio occurs are Romans 5:2-5; I Corinthians 13:13; Galatians 5:5, 6; and I Thessalonians 5:8.

Verse 3 spotlights three marks of a healthy local

church. First, it will be marked by the work produced by faith. Only faith that inspires works is a living, saving force.

Next, the labor of love. In our day this phrase has become a cliché for work we do without any expectation of reward. This term originally was tinged with sacrifice, including the notions of toil and fatigue. Maclaren says, "Love is the only principle that will carry us through the fatigue, difficulties and oppositions which rise against us."

Finally, there is endurance inspired by hope. Findlay points out that this is not the resignation of the passive sufferer so much as the fortitude of the stouthearted soldier. Such endurance and patience carries the Christian warrior in the hope of victory through the long day's march and conflict.

1:4 Because of their response to the Good News, Paul can say that the Thessalonians are chosen. This word is a compound derived from the preposition "out" and the verb "I say." Its meaning is "to select from a group." For example, in the Old Testament, God selected a people (the Jews) to serve as a channel of His grace to the world.

In the New Testament the word is used of Jesus' selection of the twelve out of a larger group of disciples (Luke 6:12-16).

The doctrine of election is often represented as the choice of a God who damns or saves according to His own whim with no regard for justice. This God is a popular straw man for some authors such as Mark Twain and Kurt Vonnegut. However, this is not the true doctrine. Election must be seen as the inscrutable mystery that it is, in light of all that is revealed in Scripture, including *our* responsibility to choose God.

1:5 Because there were those in Thessalonica who were slandering Paul, the apostle reminded the church members of those days when they first heard the Gospel proclamation. That image of Paul in their minds would offset the criticism of those who sought to discredit Christ's messenger.

For Discussion

1. How do you answer someone who says that faith, hope, and love are nice sounding, but easily evaporating words?

2. Can you name examples of individuals in whom you have seen faith, love, and patience? What were they actually like?

3. What lessons can be learned from the Thessalonians regarding Christian living? How do these lessons apply to your life right now?

Window on the Word

You People Are Different

Everett Martin had a dream. This general manager of an Atlanta television station could envision hundreds of volunteers fanning out through the metro area with boxes of food and Christmas gifts for needy families. The men and women would leave Bibles and Bible study pamphlets, and share their faith as they had opportunity. Each visit would be a demonstration of Christian love in action.

Martin's dream came true. Christian business people and a special telethon raised $25,000 for the project. When it came time to deliver the packages, hundreds of Christians showed up to stuff boxes and deliver the goods. More than 1,000 families were served, and visitors were frequently asked to have prayer.

A police officer who watched the busy workers was astonished at their evident dedication. He told them several times, "You people are different."

Do your friends and neighbors see the difference Christ makes in your life?

2

Model Christians

Truth to Apply: I am called to be an imitator of Christ, and a model for other believers.

Key Verses: You became imitators of us and of the Lord. And so you became a model to all the believers (I Thess. 1:6a, 7a).

Dr. Eleanor Chestnut served the Savior as a missionary doctor in China during the last century. In His name, she ministered to the sick in body and the ill in soul. On one occasion, a beggar was badly burned, and it was diagnosed he'd need a skin graft to stay alive. But people would not give their skin; they thought the beggar wasn't worth it. The next morning, however, hospital aides discovered the graft had been made. It was unknown where the skin had come from—until Dr. Chestnut was seen *limping!*

Robert G. Lee, powerful preacher of recent years, preached a sermon on "Making Disciples by Righteous Living." In it he declared, "We influence others—win them to our way of thinking and living—by what we are. What a person *is* is the sun which radiates the warmth of life for other lives, or the frozen orb from which rises darkness and death for others."

Do you agree that a good case could be built for "evangelization by example"? What would be the strengths of this approach? Weaknesses?

Background/Overview: *I Thessalonians 1:6-10*

After sharing his prayers with these believers and telling them that he is thankful for their faith, hope, and love (the evidence of their true conversion), Paul goes on to observe further evidence of conversion. They imitated the apostles and the Lord, and in spite of suffering, they, too, became models for other believers in outlying regions. He finishes the chapter with a note on the coming of Christ to rescue them from the coming wrath.

Light on the Text

1:6 "You became imitators of us and of the Lord." One of the most profound and important truths in the Christian world view is the principle of imitation. Here the apostle commends the Thessalonian believers because they have become imitators of the apostles and of the Lord. Notice that the emphasis is on the apostles first and the Lord second. Why this order? Surely Paul did not think he was a better example than the Lord Jesus!

Still, he must have had a reason. If we think about the question for a while it seems apparent that Paul is simply indicating the natural process of spiritual development which these new Christians must have experienced—learning to follow the example of Christ by first following the example of the mature believers around them. This kind of human interaction is essential to spiritual growth in new believers.

It might be helpful to do a word study using the term "imitator" and its verb form "to imitate."

First, one must find the words and where they appear in the Bible. A concordance like *Strong's Exhaustive Concordance* tells us where the Greek words are found.

On the following page is a list of the locations where various forms of the Greek word for "imitate" are found. Look up the references and paraphrase the way the word is used in that particular context.

I Cor. 4:16:

Eph. 5:1:

I Thess. 1:6:

I Thess. 2:14:

II Thess. 3:9:

Heb. 6:12:

Heb. 13:7:

III Jn. 11:

On the basis of these passages, what are your observations about the meaning of the word "imitate"?

1:7 The imitators became the imitated. The word translated "model" is the root for our word "type," as in typeface—that which makes an impression on something else. It was used to describe the manufacture of money. An artisan would strike a piece of precious metal, forcing it into the pattern of a coin.

1:8 The words "rang out" may refer to the sound of a trumpet or perhaps the peal of thunder. This was not a secret thing!

1:9 "You turned to God from idols." The Thessalonian believers followed the normal and expected experience of conversion. They turned from idols to serve the living and true God. The idea is fundamental to the Bible. Those who will follow God must turn from evil. For example, in the Old Testament we find (in Jeremiah 18:8), "If that nation I warned repents of [turns from] its evil, then I will relent," and in Isaiah 55:7, "Let the wicked forsake his way and the evil man his thoughts. Let him turn to the Lord, and he will have mercy on him, and to our God, for he will freely pardon."

Paul's own experience of conversion was dramatic. On the road toward Damascus he saw the Lord, and his life was changed. Yet Paul's conversion was unusual in that he received a special visitation from Christ Himself in the light and the sound. Most people are converted through the witness of others.

In any case, the point is that never in the Bible is there any indication that a person can make some sort of superficial "profession" without making a serious attempt to turn from evil. This is true repentance.

"To serve the living and true God." What would this conversion entail for relatively sophisticated pagans in the first century? For one thing, it would mean a new understanding of the whole order of the world. Instead of having to rely on arbitrary and undependable gods who could not be trusted, they would now be able to believe what they were told. To those of us who are used to thinking of God as consistent it requires a bit of imagination to appreciate such a world view. For example, in Homer's *Iliad* (a poem that formed the basis of Greek and Roman education), Zeus, the chief god, lies, changes his mind, and is willing to deceive almost anyone he can to get what he wants. Even the pagan philosophers were appalled by the spoiled, childish gods.

1:10 "To wait for his Son from heaven." The conversion these people experienced was positive, not merely negative. They had hope. On the other hand, the pagan teaching about life after death was not comforting. Most people had heard stories of some sort of existence in the realm of the god of the underworld, Hades. This existence was terrible because persons lived there as disembodied spirits. In Homer's *Odyssey,* Achilles, one of the great heroes of Greece, is visited by Odysseus and tells his old comrade that he would rather be alive as the most humble person in the world instead of the king of the dead. As you read inscriptions on graves in the pagan world you are stricken by the hopelessness of those left behind. They usually follow a pattern such as this: "I, Titus, centurion of the XX Legion, raise this marker in the memory of my beloved Lucinda. My tears shall fall forever." There is never any mention of a hopeful reunion or resurrection. There is only the sense of utter desolation.

"Who rescues us from the coming wrath." God's wrath is not a popular topic in these days of always trying to be positive. But God is rightly angry with humankind for its willfulness.We are not, perhaps, as bad as we can be, but we are surely less than we ought to be. Thus when Christ comes, He comes in wrath against those who do not obey His word. Given our experience of human behavior, it appears that such an intervention is needed to set things right. Part of this is judgment. Happily, another part is deliverance from wrath on the basis of Christ's death.

For Discussion

1. Share some examples of experiences you have had with the principle of imitation.

2. Do you know of a model church? Make a list of the characteristics you think a model church should have.

3. What is the nature of an idol? Think of some examples in your own life.

Window on the Word

Help Them Carry Their Burdens

In his excellent book *The Master Plan of Evangelism* (Revell), Robert Coleman provides this incisive thought about discipling others:

"What perhaps is the most difficult part of the whole process of training is that we must anticipate their problems and prepare them for what they will face. This is terribly hard to do, and it can become exasperating. It means that we can seldom put them out of our mind. Even when we are in our private meditations and study, our disciples will still be in our prayers and dreams. But would a parent who loves his children want it any other way? We have to accept the burden of their immaturity until such time as they can do it for themselves. To take the attitude, at least in the early stages of their development, that they can handle completely on their own whatever comes along is inviting disaster. We must be sensible. As their guardian and advisor we are responsible for teaching our spiritual children how to live for the Master."

3

A Transparent Life

Truth to Apply: My testimony is enhanced through honest sharing of my life with others.

Key Verses: You know we never used flattery, nor did we put on a mask. We loved you so much that we were delighted to share with you not only the gospel of God but our lives as well . . . (I Thess. 2:5a, 8).

The story is told of Oliver Cromwell, the Puritan, who was having his portrait painted. The artist wanted to flatter him by leaving off his warts. But Oliver insisted that the picture show him "warts and all."

Suppose you are in a bad mood, and your friend calls. Do you try to cover up your feelings with spiritual froth? Or do you say the truth: "I am having a bad day."? Why?

Background/Overview: *I Thessalonians 2:1-16*

Paul reminds the Thessalonians of his successful preaching in their city after the troubles at Philippi. He also reminds them that the missionaries came in the power of God—not with impure motives. He concludes by reminding the believers of their acceptance of the Word of God and the suffering it brought about.

We should be aware that the world is full of people who want to control or cheat others with fine sounding words. Such was the case in the first century, and Paul was accused of being such a person. He responded by reminding the believers of their experience with him. He had been honest and aboveboard. He had shared his life and feelings openly. They knew him. The charges were manifestly false.

Light on the Text

2:1 Paul tells the Thessalonians that his visit to them "was not a failure" (vs. 1). The apostle declares that when he came to Thessalonica, he saw results. In the Greek, "was" is in the perfect tense, indicating action that took place in the past and which continues on into the present. Paul's visit was still bearing results!

This success was not necessarily in terms of what the world calls success. Like Paul, we must use God's standard alone. For example, in American life, the bigger the better. But it is not necessarily true that the bigger church is the better church. We ought not despise growth, but we ought not assume that a church with many members is spiritually healthy for that reason alone.

2:2 Paul recalls his experience at Philippi (Acts 16:11-40). There he preached to women who met at a place of prayer. As a result, Lydia was converted. Shortly thereafter Paul met a slave who told fortunes. She followed him, crying out,"These men are servants of the Most High God." Paul was grieved and commanded the spirit to come out of her. After her owners discovered that their means of profit was gone, they brought charges that these Jews had stirred up trouble by importing foreign customs.

Paul and Silas were beaten without a trial, and thrown in jail. During the night, as they were singing psalms, God freed them with an earthquake. As a result, the jailer and his household were converted. The next day the magistrates discovered that they had beaten and jailed Roman citizens. Out of fear, they freed them and asked them to leave the city.

Paul states that he spoke to the Thessalonians about the Gospel of God "in spite of strong opposition" (vs. 2). Because this word originally referred to a contest in the arena, Paul is referring to a genuine struggle, not simply a game. In the classical world, athletic contests often ended in death. Remember that Paul and Silas had been beaten and jailed in Philippi because they had interfered with a fortune-teller's business.

2:3 The word here translated "appeal" is rendered "exhortation" in the ASV. Its original meaning is "to call to one's side to help." It is a word related to John's favorite word for the Holy Spirit, "Comforter."

"Error" can sometimes mean "deceit" (as it is translated in the KJV), but here it simply means the state of being incorrect or factually wrong. The point is that the New Testament has a high regard for truth. A common criticism one hears from those who do not accept the Bible is that the writers of this time were not interested in accuracy. This is usually accompanied by some instance of obvious error, such as the Ptolemaic system, in which the earth was described as the center of the universe.

While it is true that classical civilizations were not as concerned with the sort of measurement that interests a technological society, their concern for truth and veracity was at least as high as ours. Here Paul claims to be accurate. What he has told the Thessalonians conforms to reality.

"Or impure motives." The word Paul uses here to defend himself against slander usually refers to sexual impurity. However, this does not seem to be a usual charge against Paul. Furthermore, in II Corinthians 2:17, we find another defense: "Unlike so many, we do not peddle the word of God for profit." The rest of the passage seems to indicate that ethical, rather than sexual, slanders were being spread.

"Nor are we trying to trick you." The image here is that of trying to catch a fish with bait. Paul has been accused of being out to trick them for his own ends. Here he denies it categorically, as he does the charge of simply being wrong, of having impure motives.

Why should such a charge arise? Because there were many teachers of philosophy wandering through the world gathering disciples for their own profit. Philosophy in this context refers to life-style, or manner of living, and not some abstract system of thought that has no meaning in real life. These "gurus" told their hearers that they knew the correct way to live and would provide their disciples with the key. Such persons are always suspect, and the charge was made that Paul and Silas were teachers of this sort.

2:4 The word "approved" means to test, with the idea of *passing* the test. In English, to test with a view to cause failure, or to disapprove, is usually understood as "to tempt." The two ideas show the difference between testing from God, which ultimately strengthens us, and the testing originating from evil powers, which tries to destroy us.

"To be entrusted with the gospel." One of the great truths that has existed in the Church from its inception is the responsibility of human beings to share the life of God with others. It is a trust not to be taken lightly.

"We are not trying to please men but God, who tests our hearts." Paul is focused on the supernatural reality that God will test our hearts, our innermost beings. God is not to be deceived by nice clothes or pleasant manners.

2:5 "You know we never used flattery." Paul returns to the theme of his behavior among the Thessalonians. He did not flatter them. He told them the truth.

There is no doubt about it, flattery works. Flattery is praising someone insincerely in order to get your own way. People, even people who should know better, respond to flattery. Consequently it is important for every Christian to follow Paul's advice to the Romans, "Do not think of yourself more highly than you ought, but rather think of yourself with sober judgment" (Rom. 12:3).

"Nor did we put on a mask to cover up greed." Paul continues the theme of his behavior by declaring his honest desire to do them well, not to gain financially from them. This was, and is, a continuing concern among all who preach and all who listen. Many people are simply in the "religion" business. Those who listen must be, as Jesus said, "shrewd as snakes."

2:7 "But we were gentle among you like a mother caring for her little children." The word translated "caring" means to warm, and thus to cherish, to care for. The word is used only here, and in Ephesians 5:29 where it refers to the care and feeding of one's own body.

The simile compares the gentleness of the apostles with a nurse who is not caring for her mistress's child but for her own. It is a strong image to describe the reality of the interpersonal relationships that existed between the apostles and the church.

2:8 "We were delighted to share with you not only the gospel of God but our lives as well." This verse is the key to Paul's success as an evangelist. He did not simply tell people God loved them; he shared himself with them. The emphasis here is on the sharing of lives, not the sharing of the Gospel. Surely Paul did not think the truth of Christ's death and resurrection for sin unimportant; however, he realized and practiced the most convincing method of reaching people—he gave them his life.

In practical terms, to give one's life one must give, first of all, time. How can unbelievers begin to know what the Gospel means if they do not have contact with believers? The practice of mass evangelism results in great disillusionment if it is not preceded and followed by personal contact. This is not an easy thing to do, but it is the first step in true, Biblical evangelism.

2:9 "Toil" is "weariness" (fatigue)."Hardship" is "painfulness" (difficult labor). Before the rising sun, Paul was up and at the work of making tents so that he would not burden the Thessalonians with his support (Acts. 18:3).

2:10 The Thessalonians, as well as God, were witnesses of how Paul, Silas, and Timothy behaved among them. "Holy" means dedicated to God. "Righteous" means conforming to the law of God. "Blameless" means others can't justly accuse, or find fault with a person.

2:11 In previous verses Paul used the image of a nursing mother to describe his relationship with the Thessalonians. Here he compares himself to a loving father.

2:12 "Encouraging." This word is often used of the comforting of the bereaved or fainthearted.

"Comforting" is from the same word found in verse 3 that means "calling to one's side to help."

"Urging" is often used in the sense of "testimony," or "witness," and thus can mean "to state the truth carefully as if under oath." It refers to the necessity of speaking strongly about issues.

2:14-16 Paul points out that the opposition is those who killed the Lord Jesus and who drove out the disciples. He declares that, unlike those who believed, these persecutors are gathering condemnation to themselves, and the wrath of God is coming on them at last.

For Discussion

1. In his self-defense against the charge of impure motives, Paul appeals to the personal experience that he and the Thessalonian believers shared. How can this method be applied in a world that depends on electronic media?

2. We can see those around us who profess to be ministers of Christ, but what can we do about those whom we only know through the printed page and through the radio or TV? Discuss this at length—we are likely to have more media preachers than "live" preachers in the years to come.

3. Some people advise new believers to break with old friends who might continue to influence them toward their old life-style. Others have argued that relationships with unbelieving friends need to be encouraged for future witnessing opportunities. What do you think?

Window on the Word

An Enlightened Prayer

A four-year-old boy decided that he'd make an attempt at reciting the prayer which he had heard in church. "And forgive us our trashbaskets," he asked, "as we forgive those who trashbasket against us."

Deliver us from gossip!

4

Know Your Enemy!

Truth to Apply: Through the power of Christ, I can face every form of spiritual opposition.

Key Verse: I was afraid that in some way the tempter might have tempted you and our efforts might have been useless (I Thessalonians 3:5).

Much has been written over the years about people who sell their souls to the Devil. The source of many of the works probably goes back to a tract in which a Dr. Faustus traded his soul to the Devil for the temporary services of a demon. Later, in renaissance England, Marlowe retold the story. In his version, Faustus was thrown into hell with the usual Elizabethan special effects: a trapdoor opened and the victim was dragged, screaming, into a smoky pit.

In the 18th century, American author Washington Irving also told the story. In *The Devil and Tom Walker,* Tom bargains away his soul and goes to hell. He gets most religious as his 20-year lease runs out, but the Devil catches him as he tries to foreclose a mortgage.

Attitudes toward the Devil gradually changed as the Christian world view became less influential. The trend has been to treat the subject lightly, even humorously, with no one ever really getting hurt. For example, in a popular broadway play, the hero trades his soul for the athletic skills to lead the Washington Senators to victory over the New York Yankees. The hero gets off because one of Satan's servants has a heart of gold.

What do you think of the way Satan is pictured in our society, in films, music, and in the increase of occult activity?

Background/Overview: *I Thessalonians 2:17—3:13*

Paul tells the Thessalonians of his concern for them, though he has had to be separated from them. He tried to come, but Satan hindered him. Consequently, he sent Timothy to encourage them in their trials. Timothy returned with a good report of the believers, for which Paul thanks God. He finishes this section with a prayer for their increase in love so that they will be holy and blameless at the Son's coming.

Paul's reference to Satan is by no means without precedent. Note some of the many places Satan is mentioned by name in the Old Testament: Job 1, 2; I Chronicles 21:1; Psalm 109:6; Zechariah 3:1, 2. In all these instances Satan is one who accuses people, godly people, before God. He is our enemy.

Light on the Text

2:17 "Intense longing." The original Greek word is almost always translated "lust" in the other places it occurs in the New Testament. That Paul uses it here indicates his passion, his great love, toward these believers. He really wants to come to see them.

2:18 "But Satan stopped us." The word translated "stopped" means "to cut into" and was used in a military context in the sense of breaking up a road, or destroying bridges.

Serving God does not make one immune to Satan's interference. Paul felt hindered. Yet while Paul himself couldn't go to see the believers, he could send Timothy. It was undoubtedly an important learning experience for Timothy. Furthermore, Paul then had the time and inclination to write the two letters that have blessed many, many people over the years. In short, God in His providence overruled the plans of Satan.

This is the case in all the events that have happened since the beginning. Humanity's fall was a terrible event. Much pain and sorrow for God and us came from it.

However, it is clear that God's solution to the problem of sin resulted in great glory for Him and great benefit for sinners. We may become children of God! God overpowers evil with good.

2:19 "Coming." The Greek word is *parousia,* meaning "presence." This Greek word is so widely used that it is on its way to becoming an English word. In the Mediterranean world it was used to describe the arrival of a king. Paul uses it here to describe the coming of the greatest of all kings, Christ Jesus.

3:3 "You know quite well that we were destined for them." "Destined" is a strong word meaning something that cannot be changed. Trials are not an option to a Christian. They are inevitable. It makes sense, after all, that if we refuse to do the evil things that are commonplace in our society we should expect some sort of negative response.

3:5 "The tempter might have tempted you." Another of Satan's titles is Tempter. The word means "to put to the test." When Satan tempts Christians, he doesn't intend for them to pass the test. He is our enemy!

3:6 "Good news." This is the same Greek word as the one used for "Gospel." The good news here was the good report Timothy brought to Paul about what was happening in Thessalonica. Thus the term originally meant any kind of good report. From this ordinary use came its special Christian sense—the good news of God's gracious salvation through Christ's death.

3:8 "Standing firm." The Greek word is a strong term meaning "to stand fast." It is not the everyday term for standing. Paul likes it enough to use it extensively:

I Corinthians 16:13, "Be on your guard; stand firm in the faith; be men of courage; be strong. Do everything in love."

Galatians 5:1, "It is for freedom that Christ has set us free. Stand firm, then, and do not let yourselves be burdened again by a yoke of slavery."

Philippians 1:27, ". . . I will know that you stand firm in one spirit, contending as one man for the faith of the gospel. . . ."

Philippians 4:1, ". . . that is how you should stand firm in the Lord, dear friends!"

II Thessalonians 2:15, "So then, brothers, stand firm and hold to the teachings we passed on to you, whether by word of mouth or by letter."

In these verses it is clear that Paul uses this term to encourage believers to resist the temptation to move away from the doctrine they received from the apostles.

Observe two points in this connection. First, the loyalty the apostle urges is to the truth of the Gospel, not to a particular organization. Second, the assumption is that we are in a spiritual battle and that one of the skills we must develop is the ability to hold the line, to stand fast.

How does one stand fast? Not simply by being an arch conservative. God's truth needs to be communicated to the world in terms the world can understand. But some things *are* changeless. We can and must stand for the truth and oppose the Wicked One on all fronts. For example, today one of those fronts is the degeneration and erosion of family life. Many need to be reminded that children who serve the Lord are a Christian's glory.

3:13 "Strengthen" means "to support." In the Middle Ages, builders discovered that a wall could be thinner and have more windows if it was supported with a buttress. Believers' hearts need to be strengthened and supported as well. The One who does it is the Lord Himself.

"Hearts." To a citizen of the first century this word did not mean the muscle in the center of the chest that pumps blood. It meant the whole person—mind, will, and emotions. We serve in a spiritual war, needing strong hearts to bear vicious spiritual attacks.

"Blameless" means the imputed virtue and holiness that we need to stand uncondemned before our God and Father. It does not mean that we are able to provide such a character for ourselves. It is by grace.

"Holy" means distinctively given to God, or dedicated to His use. In the Old Testament, an animal destined for sacrifice was dedicated to God; it was holy. The priests and Levites who had special responsibilities were also holy in the same sense. Paul indicates a state rather than a process.

"Holy ones" can mean either angels or saints who have gone before. Angels are called holy ones in the Greek Old Testament. In Psalm 89:5 we read, "The heavens praise your wonders, O Lord, your faithfulness too, in the assembly of the holy ones." Daniel 4:13 says, "I looked, and there before me was a messenger, a holy one, coming down from heaven."

Since both groups are associated with the Second Coming, it seems unnecessary to require one or the other as the only meaning. Again Paul finishes a section by reminding the believers of the fact of the return of the Lord Jesus.

For Discussion

1. Have you ever had an experience in which you felt the "invisible battle"?

2. What effect do popular occult movies have on people's understanding of the Devil?

3. Providence does not mean there will be no evil in the world. But what *does* it mean?

Window on the Word

Providence

"God's works of providence are his most holy, wise, and powerful, preserving and governing all his creatures and all their actions" (*Westminster Shorter Catechism*).

This statement of the doctrine of providence is a brief and powerful statement of what Christians have believed since the first century. We believe that God is in control of the situation. What happens in day-by-day events is not a surprise to God. He governs all.

Of course, we must realize that this government is not the flawed and broken government of a human political party. Though it is most holy and wise, the stream of events is not always easy to understand. We know of people who love and serve God, yet suffer many trials. On the other hand, we know of confessed scoundrels who prosper. How do we explain these things?

One thing is clear. We cannot understand everything. We can expect to be faced with many a mystery. We don't know why disasters strike. We don't know why so many people have to suffer unjustly. But we do know that God's providence is real and that He never leaves us to face the difficulties alone.

5

Staying Pure

Truth to Apply: God holds me responsible for the wise use of my sexuality.

Key Verse: For God did not call us to be impure, but to live a holy life (I Thessalonians 4:7).

We have no choice in the matter! Sexual purity is required for all who follow Christ. Christians believe and teach that sexual pleasures are to be limited to those who are willing to commit themselves to marriage. Not for as long as our love shall last, but for as long as we both shall live! Men and women are designed by God to live as man and wife, to raise children in the nurture and admonition of the Lord. It is one of the prime reasons for existence.

A local television station did a report on the singles scene since the epidemic of AIDS and herpes first came to broad public attention. Many of the people interviewed said they were now afraid to go out looking for casual partners. The same worry fills the papers and TV talk shows. What are we Christians to make of this? Should we be happy? Should we be sad? What steps should we take to help our young people become aware of the issues and to deal with them?

Background/Overview: *I Thessalonians 4:1-12*

In the first part of the chapter, Paul urges the new converts to be careful about themselves, to live a life of moral purity, to be "useful to the Master" (II Tim. 2:21). Then he reminds them of their relationship with other Christians. Love should be the family tie that binds hearts together in Christ. Finally, he warns them about their relationship to the world. Their conduct ought to be exemplary, their dealings honest, and their work self-sustaining. If the character of their faith is reflected in such holy patterns of life, his work indeed will not have been in vain.

Paul urges the Thessalonians to continue to please God, and reminds them of the requirements for sexual purity and faithfulness in marriage. In 4:1-8 he speaks to them about restraining sexual passion, reminding them that holiness is God's will, that God has called them to holiness, and that anyone who despises holiness rejects "not man . . . but God."

In verses 10 and 11, Paul exhorts them to neglect none of the ordinary duties of life under the pretext of spirituality.

Light on the Text

4:1, 2 "Live in order to please God, as in fact you are living." Note that it *is* possible to please God. If we are not careful, we will allow Satan's lie (that we cannot do anything right) to confuse us.

4:3 "It is God's will that you should be holy." "Holy" is the word for sanctification, or dedication to divine service. "Sanctification is a work of God's grace, whereby . . . they, whom God hath . . . chosen to be holy, are, in time, through the powerful operation of his Spirit . . . renewed . . . after the image of God" (*Westminster Larger Catechism*). To be holy does not mean that we become weird, or strange, or nonhuman. It means that we think about God and His guidance in whatever we do.

This is not a burden any more than it is a burden for a man who loves his wife to do things that cost him time and trouble to make her happy. It is a burden that lovers share. Sheep devoted to Temple service ("sanctified") were no less sheeplike. In the same way, people who are holy are no less human.

"That you should avoid sexual immorality." Here Paul spells out what he expected the believers to do. They should not pay vows to Aphrodite. They should not visit prostitutes. They should control their sexual drives, expressing them only within the marriage relationship. Yet there is no question of Victorian fear and repression of sexual activity in a Biblical life-style. A quick reading of the Song of Songs will make that very clear. God is no prude!

A psychiatrist whose practice is made up of mostly Christians says that Christians are as sexual as any other population in the world. But too many have grown up in situations where purity meant denial of sex. Christians need to become comfortable with their own sexuality, and Christian parents need to develop the skills to talk to their children about this topic as much as any other.

4:4 "Control his own body." There is some question about the word here translated "body" because it is literally "vessel." In some commentators' minds the word should mean "wife," not "body." They argue that a wife was a vessel for the husband. While there is some evidence that this could be the original meaning, the only other instance of this usage in the Bible would be I Peter 3:7 (where the wife is called the "weaker vessel" [KJV]).

But this I Peter passage actually has nothing to do with the wife being the husband's vessel. They are *both* vessels of the Spirit, she being called the weaker. ("Weaker" presumably meant *physically weaker.*) Thus, Paul apparently uses the term *vessel* to mean the body, male or female. We are to control this body in such a way as to be holy and honorable, that is, in sexual restraint. This is not to say that we are to deny the reality of human sexuality. After all, God created us as physical beings with sexual drives. The drive is good, having been given by God, but it must be expressed in accordance with God's guidelines. Sex is for marriage and all that that commitment involves.

4:5 "Not in passionate lust like the heathen." Verse 5 shows an essential difference between believer and pagan. The "heathen" indulge their lustful appetites because they do not know God. Christians, because they know God, can live differently. This is Paul's key point.

First-Century Morality

The pagan world of the first century was full of promiscuity. It was also a "man's world" in that the double standard was a widely accepted norm. The mores of the time were largely based on Homer's poetry, (similar to the way the Bible influenced Elizabethan England). For example, in *The Odyssey*, Odysseus is separated from his wife for 20 years. During this time she runs his house, raises his son, and remains faithful. Odysseus, on the other hand, has relations with whomever he pleases.

It was not unusual for a man to keep his wife on the second floor while visiting the servant girls on the ground floor. There was no stigma attached to him. However, if he was married to a strong woman with a strong family, he sometimes behaved better.

Pagan society included worship of fertility goddesses. "Worship" is perhaps the wrong word, since their rites included temple prostitution. Corinth was notorious for such practices. The mystery religions flourished at this time, but little detail is known about their rites, except that some of them included much sexual activity.

Some philosophers, and small groups of both pagan and Jewish traditions (like the Jewish Essenes), preached and practiced celibacy, but they were a distinct minority. All in all, the classical world needed the truth Paul was preaching to the Thessalonians: Be pure!

4:6 "Punish men for all such sins." They didn't realize that such things were punishable because they were without personal knowledge of God.

4:8 "He who rejects this instruction does not reject man but God." We live in an age when many claim the Christian view of sex is too restrictive; they seek "freedom." However, Paul disagrees. A Christian sexual ethic is not a human set of rules, but God-given guidelines for our own protection. Thus Paul can state that people who live in sexual immorality may expect miserable results—usually the natural consequences (disease, broken families, guilt) of their misdeeds.

4:9, 10 Christians are people of love. Naturally, they will show love to their brothers and sisters in Christ, but they will also seek to help others in need. Though Paul emphasizes the marital relationship in this passage, we must not forget those who are single. For example, consider the needs of the single parent. What an opportunity for loving ministry! There are many, many broken families with children growing up in an unbalanced environment. Let us prepare ourselves to minister to the single parents who are trying to cope with raising a child alone.

It is a great thing to be able to help fellow Christians, but we can do more than that. Paul and Silas gave the people their own souls. Having given so much, they had an audience that would listen to them.

4:11 "Ambition to lead a quiet life." The Greek word for "ambition" is used in Romans 15:20, "It has always been my ambition to preach the gospel where Christ was not known," and in II Corinthians 5:9, "So we make it our *goal* to please him."

The phrase here is somewhat paradoxical, putting "ambition" and "quiet" together. Paul seems to be saying "stir yourselves up to be still." The paradox would no doubt appeal to the Greek mind. His point is that we should go about our lives in a way that honors God so that when the Lord comes again we will be doing our duty. What better way for the steward to greet the Lord!

"To mind your own business." Apparently there were some who were interfering in the work of the church instead of simply paying attention to the things in which they were trained and skilled.

"To work with your hands." Paul enjoins honest work. He dignifies all labor by making it a religious duty. This does not result in religion being the opiate of the people, as Marx suggested. Instead, it places a value on work that encourages all workers to do their best.

4:12 "So that your daily life may win the respect of outsiders." The word translated "respect" more literally means "in good form." It is used in reference to honest financial transactions, but also may include decency in domestic, social, and political affairs (A. T. Robertson, *Word Pictures in the New Testament*). The only other places it occurs in the New Testament are Romans 13:13 ("Let us walk honestly"), and I Corinthians 14:40 ("But everything should be done in a fitting and orderly way").

For Discussion

1. Some Christians teach that human sexuality should only be used in order to generate children. What is your opinion? Consider the Song of Songs and Hebrews 13:4.

2. In light of this passage, how should the believer differ from the unbeliever in sexual behavior?

3. There are several terrible diseases associated with sexual promiscuity. Are these a judgment from God?

Window on the Word

Christians Who Know

"Christians, contrary to most contemporary opinion, are the people who know the truth about sex. They have learned this truth because they have faced the prior question of the truth about God and about themselves . . . Christians know that sex is good and beautiful, not some mistake of evolution or goof of God." (Douglas Dickey, "The Truth About Sex"; *His*.)

6

The First to Rise

Truth to Apply: By my words and attitudes, I can express my assurance of eternal life.

Key Verse: After that, we who are still alive and are left will be caught up with them in the clouds to meet the Lord in the air. And so we will be with the Lord forever. Therefore encourage each other with these words (I Thessalonians 4:17, 18).

He was young. He had a wife and a child. He also had vasculitis—a disease related to arthritis. He sickened shortly after Christmas, went into a coma, and in March, when spring was just beginning to come, he died. He was no great saint. He was not a national figure. He was no great preacher. He was an ordinary guy with his share of common human frailties. But he was a Christian.

Death brings terrible loneliness and helplessness, and, as a Christian doctor once said, "Everyone's patient finally dies." Though no one can avoid death, those who follow Christ need not grieve like those who have no hope.

What comfort could you give to the young man's family? How would you go about it?

Background/Overview: *I Thessalonians 4:13-18*

Paul is concerned that the Thessalonian believers are ignorant about what happens at death. To keep them from the hopeless grieving of the unbelievers, he teaches truths of comfort and encouragement. Jesus rose from the dead, and He will bring the dead with Him at His return. Furthermore, those left alive will be caught up to meet the Lord in the air.

Light on the Text

4:13-15 "We do not want you to be ignorant." Sometimes ignorance may be bliss, but this is not true in the spiritual realm. What we do not know may leave us confused, may cost us our peace, and may even be the cause of our destruction. Paul uses this phrase in I Corinthians 10:1 to let the Corinthian believers know that while all the people of Israel saw the miracles in the wilderness, not all pleased God. It is a phrase that introduces an important new idea, as it also does here. The phrase appears again in I Corinthians 12:1 to introduce Paul's discussion of spiritual gifts.

Paul did not want these new converts to be ignorant. Such ignorance would not only rob them of their peace, but destroy their testimony of faith in Christ, especially if they grieved over the death of a loved one like those who had no hope. If indeed they believed in Christ's death and resurrection, then certainly they should trust that God would take care of those who died.

"Those who fall asleep." Why does Paul speak of death as sleep? The figure goes back to the Old Testament. God said to David, through Nathan the prophet, "Thou shalt sleep with thy fathers" (II Sam. 7:12, KJV). The psalmist cried out, "Consider and hear me, O Lord my God: lighten mine eyes, lest I sleep the sleep of death" (Ps. 13:3, KJV). This use of "sleep" may have developed as a euphemism (a word that sounds better than another word) because of the apparent state of the deceased ("She looks like she is sleeping"), but certainly in the New Testament the word takes on a deeper significance. Death is like sleep, for it is not a permanent termination. The one who goes to sleep expects to awaken in glory. Jesus also used the figure to refer to the deceased Lazarus (Jn. 11:11). But His use is full of the irony that John is so fond of. Jesus tells His disciples that Lazarus is asleep; they think he is resting and will get better. Jesus then tells them bluntly he is dead. Yet he is not truly dead. In a very unique way Lazarus was asleep. He was waiting for Jesus to come and call him out of the grave!

"Or to grieve like the rest of men, who have no hope." Paul is not suggesting that normal mourning be suppressed by a false spirituality. He believes quite strongly in expressing emotions. Grieving is a normal and God-given process. We are not necessarily closer to God when we pretend that we have no feelings or concern about the death of a loved one. Remember that Jesus wept over Lazarus.

Yet Paul wants all believers to know that there is life beyond the grave and that the ones who die in Christ are separated from us only for a brief while. We who believe are not ignorant nor are we without hope. This hope distinguishes us from those who have no real comfort in their grieving. One only has to attend a funeral where hope is absent to realize the horror. Let us thank God for His grace.

"The coming of the Lord." The term Paul uses in this passage to refer to Christ's return is *parousia,* meaning "presence," or "arrival." It designates the coming of a ruler. Jesus is coming again, and this time He is coming as King!

When Jesus ascended into Heaven, two men in brilliantly shining apparel stood by the watching disciples and announced to them that "This same Jesus, who has been taken from you into heaven, will come back in the same way you have seen him go into heaven" (Acts 1:11). From that moment on, the return of Jesus became "the blessed hope" of the Church. The early Christians proclaimed it, rejoiced in it, and anxiously awaited it.

"Will certainly not precede those who have fallen asleep." Paul tells the believers his special revelation, that is, the dead will participate in Christ's return and will initially precede those who are still alive at His coming.

4:16 "For the Lord himself will come down from heaven." Here we have one of the few descriptions of the Second Coming. Yet, it gives few specifics. The Lord is coming; He is coming out of Heaven with a loud command, with the voice of the archangel, and with the trump of God, to raise the dead.

"Loud command." This is a loud shout, as in the KJV. The Greek word was used in Paul's day to describe the shout given to rowers to keep time, or the shout of an officer to his men, or a hunter to his dogs.

"The voice of the archangel." The shout of God will be joined with the voice of the archangel. This is not very clear. Michael is the only archangel mentioned in the New Testament (Gabriel is called an angel).

"The trumpet call of God." This seems to be very like the trumpet mentioned in I Corinthians 15:51, 52, "but we will all be changed—in a flash, in the twinkling of an eye, at the last trumpet. For the trumpet will sound, the dead will be raised imperishable, and we will be changed." Trumpets were associated with God's activity in the Old Testament, as in Joel 2:1, "Blow the trumpet in Zion; sound the alarm on my holy hill. Let all who live in the land tremble, for the day of the Lord is coming. It is close at hand—" Apparently the trumpet is an indicator of God's presence.

"The dead in Christ will rise first." Here is the answer to the worry of the new believers, that their loved ones would not be able to join in the celebration of the coming of the Lord. Not so, says the apostle. They shall rise first, before all the saints meet the Lord in the air.

4:17 "Caught up." The original Greek word means "to seize," "to carry off by force"—a snatching away, perhaps by angels, to meet our Lord in the air. The word "rapture" comes from the Latin form of this word.

"In the air." In the first century, the air was often thought to be the abode of demons or devils. That the saints will meet the Lord there may be an indication of the demons' total defeat.

4:18 "Encourage each other." This, of course, is the main point of the discussion of the Second Coming. We who are still alive ought to comfort one another with the teaching found here. This comfort should encourage us to be committed disciples while we still have time. We see dimly now, but we know this: that believers will finally be reunited with those who have gone before, and that at the end of all things Christ will return for us.

The Second Coming

What does I Thessalonians teach about the Second Coming? It teaches us that the return of Jesus Christ will be sudden and unexpected, as the coming of a thief in the night. No one knows the time or the season, but all should live in a state of readiness. When He does come, those believers who have died, and those who are yet alive, will meet Him in His descent from Heaven. He will not come meekly as He did in His first advent, but will come as a ruler with a shout of command. Though it is not explicitly stated, the greatest lesson we can derive from these teachings is that God remains in control of history. Because His sovereignty is sure, history is moving toward a certain consummation. We do not know when, and we do not need to know when, but a day is coming on which He will write the last word of human history on earth.

For Discussion

1. Sometimes a discussion of the Second Coming starts heated theological discussion. Have you ever had such a discussion? How did you feel afterward?

2. Death is, and always has been, a difficult reality for all people, Christian or not, to face. If you have dealt with the death of a loved one, how did you find comfort in your grief? Who was most helpful to you? Why?

3. What should bereaved Christians expect from their pastor? From their church?

Window on the Word

Holy Sonnet

Death be not proud, though some have called thee
Mighty and dreadful, for thou art not so;
For those whom thou think'st thou dost overthrow,
Die not, poor death, nor yet canst thou kill me;
From rest and sleep, which but thy pictures be,
Much pleasure; then from thee much more must flow.
And soonest our best men with thee do go,
Rest of their bones, and soul's delivery.
Thou art slave to fate, chance, kings, and desperate men,
And dost with poison, war, and sickness dwell.
And poppy or charms can make us sleep as well,
And better than thy stroke; why swell'st thou then?
One short sleep past, we wake eternally,
And death shall be no more; Death, thou shalt die.

—John Donne

7

The Day of the Lord

Truth to Apply: My manner of life should indicate that I am ready for the Lord's return.

Key Verse: Now, brothers, about times and dates we do not need to write to you, for you know very well that the day of the Lord will come like a thief in the night (I Thess. 5:1, 2).

It was a large, well-known Bible college, and the chapel speaker was an expert on prophecy. He was involved in current events and was especially anxious to influence the government to discontinue a certain foreign aid program. He felt that the program helped a repressive government. To motivate the audience, he used a current event as an indicator that the Day of the Lord was at hand. He said, "I know that setting such a date is wrong, but . . . ."

If you were a student, how would you react?

Background/Overview: *I Thessalonians 5:1-11*

Paul reminds the believers that the Day of the Lord will come suddenly, like a thief in the night, or like the onset of labor pains. He goes on to say that the Thessalonians are not asleep in darkness, but are sons (and daughters) of light, and should be sober and aware. They should be dressed in the armor of faith, love, and hope. They are not appointed for wrath, but for salvation; therefore, they should encourage one another.

Light on the Text

5:1 "Times and dates." The two original words show a difference in meaning that is difficult to see in our language. "Times" is the word from which our word "chronology" is derived. It is a description of duration. However, "dates" is something different. It is duration in its qualitative aspect: "It is the right time"; "It is an idea whose time has come." The point Paul is making is that the believers know something about the chronology of the Second Coming (when it will happen in relation to other end time events), and the nature of the era when it is ready to appear.

5:2 "For you know very well." In I Thessalonians, Paul frequently reminds readers of their own knowledge. There is great irony here; they know perfectly that they don't really know when the day will arrive, for it will arrive like a thief, or like labor pangs.

"The day of the Lord." This expression is ancient. It refers to the time of God's bringing human history to a climactic close. It is used most often to refer to the entire scheme of events in the end times, including the return of Christ, the resurrection of the dead, the judgment and rewards, the new Heaven and earth. According to Amos 5:18, 19 it will be a day of judgment: "Woe to you who long for the day of the Lord! . . . That day will be darkness, not light. It will be as though a man fled from a lion only to meet a bear. . . ."

In the New Testament, we see it in a number of places. For example:

I Corinthians 5:5, "Hand this man over to Satan, so that the sinful nature may be destroyed and his spirit saved on the day of the Lord."

II Peter 3:10, "But the day of the Lord will come like a thief. The heavens will disappear with a roar; the elements will be destroyed by fire, and the earth and everything in it will be laid bare."

However, the day is not simply a day of judgment. In Ephesians 4:30, Paul calls it "the day of redemption." Those who follow the Lord need not fear it like those who have set themselves against His rule.

Understanding Biblical Figures of Speech

The Bible employs many kinds of figures of speech. One of the most important is the comparison. Comparison figures of speech work by drawing the reader's attention to the similarities between two very unlike things. Naturally, they will not be taken literally. For example, Robert Burns' "My love is like a red, red rose" does not mean that his girl friend has green, thorny legs and her feet are covered with fertilizer! He means that as the red rose is a paragon of beauty, so she is also.

There are two ways to compare unlike things. An *explicit* comparison, normally using "like" or "as," is called a simile. An *implied* comparison identifies the two things by equating them with each other, using a form of "is." This is called a metaphor. Both types are widely used in the Bible. For example:

Simile: "Is not my word like fire, declares the Lord, and like a hammer that breaks a rock in pieces?"

Metaphor: "You are a lion's cub, O Judah."

Whenever we encounter these figures of speech we must interpret them by noting the point or points of comparison and ignoring the differences. When the Lord says His "word is like a consuming fire" He does not mean that it requires asbestos paper for it to be written! He means that the Word purges away all excuses in the day of reckoning. This is the first step in interpreting figures of speech: look at the points of likeness, not the differences.

"Like a thief in the night." This simile describes the Lord's coming at the last day. Like all similies, it compares two unlike things. One is the thief who breaks into houses after dark. The other part of the comparison is the Day of the Lord. This is truly a comparison of two unlike things. How is the Day of the Lord like a thief? The key point of comparison is the unexpected nature of the event. Thieves do not send messages telling victims of their plans. So the Day of the Lord will come without warning.

5:3 "While people are saying, 'Peace and safety,' destruction will come on them suddenly." The attitude of the wicked is clearly described. Though they expect to go on forever in their wicked ways, they will be overtaken by sudden judgement. The word translated "safety" means "unshakable," indicating the folly of those who are unprepared.

"As labor pains on a pregnant woman." Paul's second simile uses the labor pains of a mother. Here the simile includes the suddenness of labor, but adds the inevitability of the birth which will complete the pregnancy. There is no possible alternative.

5:4 "But you, brothers, are not in darkness." Paul again expresses a settled conviction that the world is divided into two groups, those who follow God and are in light, and those who do not follow God, and consequently, are in darkness. The darkness in question is spiritual, of course. Paul is not even concerned with intellectual or cultural darkness. Often people make the mistake of equating culture with true spirituality. It isn't so.

5:5 "You are all sons of the light." In Paul's world, to be a son of something was a metaphor meaning that one had the qualities of that thing. A son of thunder was characterized by loudness. Here a son of light is characterized by light. The term was also used by the Essenes (a very conservative Jewish sect) living in the

Qumran community by the Dead Sea during that same time. One of their scrolls is entitled "The War of the Sons of Light with the Sons of Darkness."

"Sons of the day." This metaphor also picks up the light-dark contrast but adds the idea that the Day of the Lord is something believers look forward to because it means their deliverance.

5:6-11 "Be alert and self-controlled." Believers need to behave like sons of light, which means that they cannot sleep spiritually or be drunk—favorite nighttime activities for the others. This is a metaphor for the current state of the world.

The command against drunkenness does not seem to be directed to believers who were fond of wine, but rather to the uncontrolled debauchery associated with drink.

"Let us be self-controlled, putting on faith and love as a breastplate." Paul takes up the image of a soldier arming for battle and connects it to the idea of self-control. He is talking of a spiritual conflict, and the defenses needed are spiritual.

Faith is trust. It is not so much an act of the intellect as an act of the will. It includes the idea of commitment to a person and a way of life. It is necessary for salvation.

"Love" is the Greek word *agape* (ah-GAH-pay). It is a deep love that is not simply an emotional attachment. On the human level, *agape* puts the other person's best interests ahead of one's own desires or welfare. The great example is the love of Christ that led Him to die for us. There is no better or more profound example.

"Hope of salvation as a helmet." Paul continues the simile by urging the believers to put on the helmet of hope. In the classical world, hope was a neutral idea meaning the expectation of either good or evil. For Old Testament writers it meant hope in God (Ps. 43:5, "Put your hope in God, for I will yet praise him, my Savior and my God").

"Build each other up." This is the main point in all of Paul's discussions concerning Christ's coming. We who are alive need to build each other up, comforting and encouraging one another with the promises of the Scripture.

For Discussion

1. Have you ever been robbed? How does the image of a thief in the night make you feel?

2. Paul uses the images of day and night, light and darkness to portray the sharp contrast between believers and unbelievers. Why? How does this image affect you?

3. The military images of breastplate and helmet indicate that we are in a spiritual battle. What does this mean in your personal life? Our national life? How closely is spiritual conflict connected to international conflict?

Window on the Word

Exobiology

A brand-new science called "Exobiology" came into being in the 1960's. This science is dedicated specifically to the study of extraterrestrial life. In laboratories, at giant radio observatories, and at esoteric symposiums, some of the world's keenest intellects are focusing on this new discipline. Someone, however, has sardonically called exobiology a science "that has yet to demonstrate that its subject matter exists."

It *will* be demonstrated at the sudden return of Christ!

8

Peace in the Church

Truth to Apply: Before jumping to conclusions, I must get the facts.

Key Verse: Test everything. Hold on to the good. Avoid every kind of evil (I Thess. 5:21, 22).

A college English teacher was approached after class by a very intense and concerned student. "Mr. Wilson, we heard some terrible things at church last night," she said. "The Federal Communications Commission is going to take all religious broadcasting from the air. There is this bill before Congress . . ."

She continued, telling about the details that had been given to her on a mimeographed handout. It urged Christians to contact their representatives and ask them to take action. "I think we should get everyone together. My church is going to make a lot of calls and get organized to defeat this."

"Well, Sue," the professor began when she paused, "I have some real questions about the truth of the charges. The FCC can't do this simply because someone complains about religious broadcasting. Freedom of speech works both ways. Look, Sue, you have to do a term paper for this course. This would be a good topic for a research paper. Why don't you do some investigation and see what turns up?"

Sue's research showed that the information given out in the church was completely wrong. There wasn't even a hint of an attempt to force religious broadcasting off the air. She was happy to be able to report the facts.

In your opinion, how much trouble could be avoided in the typical church if members were more careful about "testing everything" and "holding on to the good"?

Background/Overview: *I Thessalonians 5:12-15*

These verses could appropriately be called Paul's Proverbs. A proverb is a special kind of universal language. Usually it is a short, pithy saying that expresses a general moral or spiritual truth (e.g., "The fear of the Lord is the beginning of wisdom").

A key characteristic of a proverb is its vividness: "An honest answer is like a kiss on the lips" (Prov. 24:26); "A whip for the horse, a halter for the donkey, and a rod for the backs of fools!" (Prov. 26:3).

To properly interpret proverbs, we must understand that they are only one side of an issue. They do not claim to be the final word. In the same way, when Paul expresses ideas in proverbial form we must not take them as the *complete* expression of God's will on the topic. We need to balance the proverb with the rest of the Scripture.

In this section Paul concludes the epistle with a series of ethical commands that are very much like the proverbs of the Old Testament. He tells the Thessalonians to respect their Christian leaders, live in peace, warn the idle, encourage the weak, respond positively, and test everything in order to hold on to the good.

Verses 12-15 seem to concentrate on what we might call the clergy-laity relationship, and verses 16-22 are a list of ethical commands mostly focused on the principle of examining and verifying truth.

Light on the Text

5:12 "Respect those who work hard among you." The church members appear to be addressed in verses 12 and 13, and the leaders in 14 and 15. One group is asked, and the other is urged. Their common faith and community are evident—Paul refers to them all as brethren.

The word translated "respect" involves knowing their true worth, and consequently to respect them. This is not the mindless following of an appealing leader. We are never to allow anyone to guide us in spiritual things without knowing how such guidance accords with Scripture. On the other hand, neither should we criticize simply because we don't like authority.

"Work hard" is from the same Greek word translated "labor" in chapter 1. It is labor that results in weariness. They do not merely show up for committee meetings and get their names applauded in church bulletins. They work!

"Over you." This is used in Paul's world to indicate a person with authority, an official. It does not appear to be used in the technical sense of a fully structured ecclesiastical organization, but it does indicate those who function in an office of real authority.

5:13 "Hold them in the highest regard in love." The members of the church are to regard their leaders in love. Paul means that they should not see them as mere authorities, but as leaders who are worthy of trust and support. No one can be an effective minister without the continual support of the congregation. It is not necessary to like everything a church leader does, but a minister should not be attacked on the basis of personal taste.

This does not preclude dealing with a leader's real faults. Neither does it mean that no suggestions or discussions should take place. Finally, it does not mean that doctrinal error is to be ignored. There are ministers who ought to be removed from office.

5:14 "Idle." This word originally meant a soldier out of step, or a unit in disarray. From this it came to mean idleness in the sense of laziness. Apparently this was quite a problem in Thessalonica.

"Encourage the timid." "Timid" is literally the "littlesouled" or the disheartened who need to be supported by others. The real gift of encouragement is in providing support for the weak while preserving their self respect.

"Help the weak." This implies holding on to someone. Those who are weak need someone to hold on to them and not let go when troubles come.

"Be patient with everyone." Though patience is not easy, it is necessary for growth into Christian maturity. Furthermore, we all do stupid and thoughtless things occasionally. This should encourage us to be patient with others, knowing full well that we ourselves will have need of their patience sooner or later.

5:16 "Be joyful always." John Wesley remarked, "Sour godliness is the Devil's religion."

Paul is not suggesting that Christians should be happy and cheerful about the bad things that happen to them. He is suggesting that, of all people, we have wonderful reasons to experience deep joy during even the most difficult times.

"Pray continually." To pray continually does not mean nonstop praying. Rather, it means pray regularly, habitually. For example, a person with a hacking cough might say "I cough all the time." But we realize that other things, like breathing and talking, will take place between coughs. In the same way, we should constantly turn our thoughts to God in prayer. Not every second, but persistently.

5:18 "Give thanks in all circumstances." In the same way that Christians pray continually, so they give thanks continually. We know that we will experience all kinds of trials in life. Yet God has control of the circumstances, and His presence never leaves us. For this we can be thankful.

5:19, 20 "Do not put out the Spirit's fire." In this verse the Holy Spirit is pictured as a flame that can be quenched. Some commentators have seen two possibilities of interpretation. Perhaps Paul is warning the people to refrain from doing anything that would hinder the external signs of the Spirit, such as the signs described in the early chapters of Acts. The second possibility is ethical: Do not impede the witness of the Spirit in the Church—the power which directs, guides, and convicts believers. Neither interpretation excludes the other. The external signs are not important in themselves except in so far as they express and promote spiritual maturity.

"Do not treat prophecies with contempt." The word "contempt" means "to make absolutely nothing of." To prophesy means to "proclaim." Normally this refers to the preaching of God's Word. However, in the early church there were apparently prophets who presented revelations concerning future events. This kind of prophesying was certainly open to abuse, and the abuses could foster contempt for the prophetic office in general. Paul warns against abuses. Clear exhortations concerning God's will (and in line with the Scriptures) should be distinguishable from wild-eyed human predictions.

5:21 "Test everything." The word has the idea of testing coins for proper gold content, and it balances the previous command to respect prophecies. Paul expects them to be wise as serpents and to check out everything that comes along. This is an important theme in the letter. Paul, in effect, supplied them with a test to his ministry among them. He reminded the believers of what he did while he was with them. Did those accomplishments qualify him for leadership and respect? He was willing to put his own behavior in the crucible for evaluation.

The principle must be worked into everyone's life. Nothing can pass without the test of Biblical fidelity. This principle does not preclude the possibility of many things being outside of Biblical pronouncements. We need not find a verse in the Bible to tell us to brush our teeth. But we can develop a solid theological framework to guide us in the ethical decisions facing us every day.

All communication has a message. The simple situation comedy that you are watching on TV has some point to make, a philosophy or world view to express. True, most of the ideas are simplistic or even trivial, but they are there. Furthermore, most of these ideas are not in agreement with a Christian world view. "Hold on to the good." After we test all that we hear, and reject or qualify it, we must keep what is good, true, just, and holy. Eat the meat and spit out the bones.

5:22 "Avoid every kind of evil." The Greek word for "kind" is translated "appearance" in the KJV. It is better translated as kind, class, or species of evil. This is not just an exhortation to abstain from things that don't look right; it's a command to leave every form of evil alone.

For Discussion

1. Respect seems to be tied to hard work. Why do you think this is so?

2. What should you do if you find you are having trouble respecting your pastor?

3. What are some ways to test everything? Have you ever been deceived by someone who claimed to be a spiritual leader?

Window on the Word

A Practical Church

One of the keys to the success of the Wesleyan revival in the 18th century was the organization of class meetings for the nurturing of the new Christians. Describing those class meetings, John Wesley wrote:

"That it may more easily be discerned whether they are indeed working out their own salvation, each society is divided into smaller companies, called *classes*, according to their respective places of abode. There are about twelve persons in every class; one of whom is styled *the leader.* It is his business, (1) to see each person in his class once a week at least, in order to inquire how their souls prosper; to advise, reprove, comfort, or exhort, as occasion may require; to receive what they are willing to give toward the relief of the poor. (2) To meet the Minister and the Stewards of the society once a week in order to inform the Minister of any that are sick, or of any that walk disorderly, and will not be reproved; to pay to the Stewards what they have received of their several classes in the week preceding; and to show their account of what each person has contributed." (*Works of John Wesley, Vol. VIII;* Zondervan.)

9

Thoroughly Holy

Truth to Apply: I am called to live a daily life of practical holiness.

Key Verse: May God himself, the God of peace, sanctify you through and through (I Thessalonians 5:23a).

An ascetic is one who practices self-denial for the purpose of becoming holy. Personal spiritual discipline is the watchword. The ascetic ideal was popular in ancient Egypt and resulted in a number of hermits and groups of monks living in the desert. Later, in the Middle Ages, strict monastic communities were organized. These communities maintained rules that normally included poverty, chastity, and obedience. Members lived simply, worked hard, and practiced various austerities.

Many ascetics refused meat and wine in their diets, and practiced fasting at regular intervals. Some monasteries limited discussion to spiritual subjects and had a reader reading sacred texts during meals. Certain monks denied themselves more than a few hours' sleep each night, or slept while sitting up. All in all, the ideal and its implementation affected many people in the history of the church. And asceticism continues, in one form or another, to this day.

To what degree is holiness dependent upon personal spiritual discipline? How, specifically, would you describe the life of holiness?

Background/Overview: *I Thessalonians 5:23-28*

The Scripture calls us to holiness! But how is a holy life actually lived out? One of the answers that has been given existed in the classical world and continues in several forms even today: Neoplatonism. It means "new platonism" and developed out of Plato's teachings. Plato taught that the world of the spirit was more important than the world of the senses.

Plato believed that God was good, and therefore the evil in the world had to be explained in some way. He chose to clear God of the responsibility of creating evil by saying that evil was based on material forms. He taught that we are evil because we are tied to bodies. Furthermore, evil exists because when God created the world He did not create it out of nothing.

Instead, God created the world out of material already in existence. Consequently, though God did the best He could with what He had to work with, the world was still full of evil because it was made of matter in addition to spirit. Thus Plato resolved the problem of evil by making God a limited being.

Neoplatonism took Plato's ideas and expanded them. A Jewish writer named Philo of Alexandria wrote a long commentary on the Old Testament explaining all the Biblical accounts as if they were expressions of Neoplatonic truth.

The Colossian gnostic-like heresy seems to have been a form of Neoplatonic thinking. Certain teachers there taught that people should deny themselves experiences of pleasure and joy, since these related to the body rather than to the spirit. Often these teachers urged severe dietary restrictions and many bodily discomforts in an effort to attain spirituality. In answer to this, Paul says: "These [rules] are all destined to perish with use, because they are based on human commands and teachings. Such regulations indeed have an appearance of wisdom, with their self-imposed worship, their false humility and their harsh treatment of the body, but they lack any value in restraining sensual indulgence" (Col. 2:22, 23).

Light on the Text

5:23 "The God of peace." Peace is a vital Biblical concept. Here Paul returns to the same theme with which he opened the letter. In Paul's thinking, peace does not simply mean the absence of conflict. Rather, it means the total well-being of the person. One who is at peace with the world is completely well-integrated. Of course, ultimately peace cannot be achieved by unaided human effort.

Peace comes from God, who is characterized by peace. We must always remember that God is continually working to bring peace to us and to the whole of creation. He is not an angry, petty person looking for one small fault to judge people. He is actively reaching out to humanity with salvation.

"Sanctify you through and through." What is here translated as "through and through" is rendered "wholly" in the American Standard Version. The idea is "reaching the end for which one has been created." It is important to see that sanctification (holiness) is our goal. But this is not the simplistic notion that a true Christian life is a continuous round of choir practice and church services. God is present in all of a Christian's life, and eternity will not be spent in something like a continual Holy Land tour. We shall have tasks to accomplish. Our growth in holiness prepares us for greater responsibility in God's Kingdom, here and in eternity.

Furthermore, to be wholly sanctified means that all parts of our lives are under God's control. How foolish is the idea that spiritual growth is in some way separate from our physical and emotional growth!

"Whole" here means "complete in all its parts." It modifies the next three words: spirit, soul, and body.

"Spirit" often refers to wind, as in John 3:8, "The *wind* blows wherever it pleases." Its use in the Scripture seems to indicate the relation between human beings and the nonmaterial world, as in John 4:24, "God is spirit, and his worshipers must worship in spirit and in truth."

"Soul" is the word from which we get "psychology." It refers to the nonmaterial part of a person. "And body" is an important part of human existence. We were designed to live in bodies. The whole point of I Corinthians 15 is the resurrection of the body. Remember, too, that Jesus had a body after His resurrection.

How Many Parts?

One of the issues that has occupied theological discussion is the nature of personhood. Does a person consist of two or three parts? There have been two main views.

The *trichotomist* position is that there are three distinct parts of the human being: body, soul, and spirit. Body is the physical part, soul contains the emotions, and spirit includes the intellect and reason. This view is often used to support the notion that the image of God in us is triune, and thus our own nature corresponds to the Trinity: Father, Son, and Holy Spirit.

Dichotomists argue that there are really only two parts to human beings: that which is physical, and that which is nonmaterial, or spiritual. The spiritual is defined as the soul, heart, emotions, and so forth.

Probably the biggest problem in the discussion is the fact that Biblical word usage does not necessarily support either position consistently. For instance, Luke 10:27 reads "Love the Lord your God with all your heart and with all your soul and with all your strength and with all your mind . . ." This verse adds "heart" and "mind" to the "soul" and "spirit" (of I Thess. 5:23) as nonmaterial aspects of human nature. Other examples could be given.

It is best to conclude that Paul does not mean to perform an analytical dissection of human physiology and psychology in I Thessalonians 5:23. He just means the whole person.

"Be kept blameless." It is possible to be kept *blameless* without being *faultless*. However, this is not because we are capable of sinlessness in the absolute sense. Notice the subject of the sentence. God does the work of holiness in our lives.

5:24 "The one who calls you is faithful." Paul is careful to ascribe the authority and the credit for the completion of the calling to God. He initiates the call, and He is faithful to bring about the good effect of salvation in our lives. We may, and often do, fail, but He who called us is faithful. It is a great comfort to rest in Him.

5:26-28 "Greet all the brothers with a holy kiss." This was the normal way of greeting people. It is strangely out of place in our more reserved society. Many have applied this command by giving a hearty handshake. It is the sort of thing that is best translated into a corresponding, but more culturally relevant, action. Paul's main concern is a physical expression of love and greeting. Let's express our love and caring in ways people can really feel.

For Discussion

1. What is God's part in our sanctification? What is ours?

2. There are many groups that encourage wholeness in human relationships. Name some of them. What is the Christian response to such groups?

3. Do you know of any current religious groups that are essentially Neoplatonic? In what ways?

Window on the Word

Holy Cops!

In an article headlined "Cops Tell How Christ Helps Them Cope," columnist Jack Mabley quotes a police officer as saying, "Four years ago when someone called me a name, I belted him. Now I ignore it and keep going. If I have to use force, I'll use force, but just enough to handle the situation." This officer belongs to the Fellowship of Christian Peace Officers, a nationwide organization of about 2,000 members in eight cities. In a typical meeting they will drink coffee, read the Bible, and talk about how the Scriptures relate to police work.

These workers have found the presence of God to have a real effect on their lives. As another officer says, "The guys notice the difference on the street. Some young offenders tell me they'd rather have me take them in than some of the other guys in the district. . . . Most policemen don't want to give up the fast life. They might think this is a form of weakness. In reality it makes you a stronger police officer." (Reported in the *Chicago Tribune*, March 1, 1977.)

10

God Is Just

Truth to Apply: I must realize that the goodness of God would have no meaning apart from His justice.

Key Verse: They will be punished with everlasting destruction and shut out from the presence of the Lord and from the majesty of his power (II Thessalonians 1:9).

"Listen, Rev. Smith, your sermon today was good, but you spent too much time talking about hell. People don't want to hear a negative message. Some people were offended because you said that hell even has religious people. Come on, everybody knows God is love. Would God send people to hell? The sales manager at my office gave me this book. I think it will help you out."

He gave the minister a volume with a bright cover. The title was *I'm Wonderful, Everyone's Wonderful: The Power of Positiveness.* On the back was a glossy picture of the author in his Beverly Hills mansion. He was tall, tanned, and terrific, with a fifteen-thousand-dollar smile.

If you were the pastor, how would you respond?

Background/Overview: *II Thessalonians 1:1-12*

The Book of II Thessalonians

Date and place of writing: A.D. 51 or 52, from Corinth.

Purpose: In the church at Thessalonica, it was erroneously believed that the Day of the Lord had already come (2:2). Paul denied such a notion. He asserted that three events have to transpire before Jesus returns. Apostasy will be rampant; the Antichrist will be revealed; God's restraining influence against evil will be removed from the world (2:3-12).

In his first epistle, Paul directed them to "study to be quiet, and to do your own business, and to work with your own hands, as we commanded you" (I Thess. 4:11, KJV). In his second letter, this instruction was amplified because some in the congregation were evidently so taken up with Christ's return that they had stopped working as they should (II Thess. 3:6-15).

Content: The situation in the church had not changed substantially since the writing of the first letter, so most of the reasons for writing had not changed much either. Only a short time had passed between the two letters. Paul writes to encourage the Thessalonians in their persecution, to exhort them to work for their living, and finally, to clear up a misunderstanding about the end times.

After his greeting (1:1, 2), Paul tells the Thessalonians of his thankfulness for them (1:3, 4). He encourages them by teaching about the Second Coming (1:5-10). He tells them that he prays for them (1:11, 12).

Paul reminds the Thessalonian believers about events that will precede the coming of the Lord (2:1-12). Again, Paul expresses his thankfulness for them, and prays for them. Then he exhorts them to adhere to his teaching (2:13-16).

Next, the apostle requests prayer and expresses his confidence to these Christians (3:1-5). He then gives directions for dealing with slothful church members (3:6-15). The epistle closes with a benediction, and Paul verifies that he has written the letter in his own hand (3:16-18).

Light on the Text

1:3 "We ought always to thank God for you." Paul is following his own injunction in I Thessalonians 5 to give thanks continually. Here he is thankful because they are growing in faith. Notice the careful personal touch. Paul calls them brothers because he cares for them.

"Because your faith is growing more and more." The characteristic of a living organism is growth. Things that are alive grow. It is true in the spiritual world as well as in the biological world. Growth should occur in every area of our lives: intellectual, physical, emotional, relational. If God has given us a mind we should continue to improve it. We should read and keep reading. Our world is changing. We need to keep up with events. True, often what we see and hear will not make us happy, but it will give us some idea of what we ought to pray for, and what we ought to write our officials about.

1:4 "We boast about your perseverance and faith." Boasting is not something that one would expect from an apostle. Yet the original wording can be translated, "we ourselves," meaning Paul boasted. Why does Paul boast? Because he was so happy that this group of believers was still following the Lord in spite of severe persecution. Boasting about the accomplishments of others is quite different from boasting haughtily about oneself.

"Perseverance" is translated "patience" in the American Standard Version. The root word is used in Hebrews 12:2 of Christ enduring the cross. They were enduring in a difficult situation. Persecution is not pleasant, yet this church was growing.

1:5 "All this is evidence that God's judgment is right." Note first that there is a need for evidence. Those who claim to follow Christ are expected to provide evidence of new birth. If we hire a landscaper to do some lawn reseeding for us and he does it, we will not take his assurance that the grass is growing if we do not, in fact, see grass. The same is true in the spiritual world. Life shows itself.

Indeed, often the first growth is small and tentative and hard to observe, but it is still necessary to see growth before one can assume spiritual life.

The fact that the believers endured persecution with an increase in faith and love is evidence of God's justice in providing them with the support necessary to endure the testing. It is important to remember that suffering is not merely optional for Christians. It is something that comes naturally with the life of faith. If we believe, it will cost us something. It may not cost us as much as it does others, but faith that results in actions will sometimes be hated by the world.

"You will be counted worthy." Faithful endurance indicates worthiness for the Kingdom of God. It is true that salvation is a gift and that we do nothing to earn it. However, it is not true that a "religious experience" is sufficient evidence that one has been truly born again. The American Puritans used to say "I hope that I have true faith." It is an abuse of the doctrine of salvation to behave as if there were no trials, no testing, no enduring to be counted worthy of the Kingdom of God.

"Kingdom of God." This important term has two aspects, present and future. In Colossians 1:13 we read, "For he has rescued us from the dominion of darkness and brought us into the kingdom of the Son he loves." This indicates that we are presently in the Kingdom of God because we are ruled by Jesus Christ. A kingdom is, after all, a political entity.

But there is also a future aspect to the Kingdom. We have the petition in the Lord's Prayer, "Your kingdom come," in which we are asking for the rule of God to be realized on the earth. Here both ideas merge. These believers are clearly under the authority of a new King, and at the same time they are waiting for the coming of the King in a physical, manifest way.

1:6 "God is just." This starts a new idea. The suffering of the Thessalonian believers will not be in vain because God is just.

To wonder about the justice of God is not unusual, nor is it forbidden. All of us question, at times, the apparent injustices in our world. The prophet Habakkuk had serious questions about God's plan and asked about them intensely. God did not say, "Be quiet and do what you are told!" No, He revealed to the prophet a further part of His plan that Habakkuk did not perceive. The book ends with a wonderful psalm of trust in God's plan.

Here Paul argues that if it is just for God to offer salvation and citizenship in His Kingdom to sinful humanity, so it is just for Him to punish those who will not accept His offer and who remain in rebellion against their Creator.

"He will pay back trouble to those who trouble you." The term "pay back" means full and due requital. It is used in Luke 14:14, where Jesus was visiting a Pharisee. He advised the host to entertain the poor who could not pay full and due payment. God would give such a payment at the resurrection of the just.

"Trouble" is translated "narrow" in Matthew 7:14. Its companion word is used in John 16:21 of birth pangs. These troublers were apparently people who went out of their way to afflict the church.

1:7 "When the Lord Jesus is revealed from heaven." The return of the Lord Jesus will result in rest for the Church as well as the punishment of the wicked.

"Revealed" is the Greek word *apocalypse*, which means "unveiling." It is the name given to the last book of the Bible.

"In blazing fire" may refer to the punishment of the wicked, or to a divine manifestation something like the manifestation of the Spirit on the day of Pentecost.

"With his powerful angels." When the King comes He will not come without attendants. These angels may be a special class of angelic beings. Like all angels, they are God's agents.

1:8 "He will punish those who do not know God and do not obey the gospel." It is clear that the objects of punishment are willfully disobedient. This is not silly or trivial condemnation. These are enemies of God by choice.

1:9 "They will be punished." The word "punished" has in view a just condemnation.

"With everlasting destruction." This is a sobering statement. Those who are enemies of God will lose all that makes life worthwhile. They will not cease to exist.

"And shut out from the presence of the Lord." This is the ultimate punishment: loss of God's presence. Since God is the source of all good things in existence, this is a terrible loss.

For Discussion

1. Americans are not used to thinking about kings. Do you think this interferes with our understanding of Christ as King? How?

2. Paul encourages the Thessalonians by teaching that God will punish their persecutors. How do you reconcile this with the command to turn the other cheek?

3. Everlasting destruction is a sobering idea. Think about it and try to explain how it is a just part of God's plan. What are the alternatives to this belief?

Window on the Word

Glimpse of Hell

The characteristic of lost souls is "their rejection of everything that is not simply themselves." Our imaginary egoist has tried to turn everything he meets into a province or appendage of the self. The taste for the *other*, that is, the very capacity for enjoying good, is quenched in him except in so far as his body still draws him into some rudimentary contact with an outer world. Death removes this last contact. He has his wish—to live wholly in the self and to make the best of what he finds there. And what he finds there is Hell. (C. S. Lewis, *The Problem of Pain*.)

11

Not Yet!

Truth to Apply: By becoming Biblically informed about the end times, I can avoid the deception of false teachers.

Key Verse: Don't let anyone deceive you in any way, for that day will not come until the rebellion occurs and the man of lawlessness is revealed, the man doomed to destruction (II Thessalonians 2:3).

There was a Bible college student who was very committed to the doctrine that at Christ's return all the believers will be taken out of the world ("raptured") before everything falls apart. It is a widely held doctrine, but this student was so taken with it that he became bothersome to his friends. When he got worse, his fellow students decided, as students will, to play a little joke on him.

They waited until he was asleep, then they laid clothes around as if the people wearing them had suddenly disappeared. They taped a news broadcast describing the sort of disaster that would happen if millions of people were suddenly removed from the world. They set up rooms with lights on and radios playing, just as if everyone had left a moment before. When all was prepared, a music major blew a blast on his trumpet to wake the victim. Everyone fled. He woke to an empty dorm. The radios were playing stories of a national disaster, the showers were running with no one in them, piles of empty clothes lay about. Needless to say, the jokers enjoyed it much more than the victim!

The joke was funny, but what about the truth it expresses? A great number of people care so much about their prophetic system that they lose sight of the reason God revealed the truth of the second coming in the first place. What is this reason?

Background/Overview: *II Thessalonians 2:1-5*

The word "millennium" comes from the Greek word for "thousand." It refers to the thousand-year reign of Christ spoken of in Revelation 20. There are three traditional millennial views:

Premillennial: This position holds that the return of Christ will come before His literal thousand-year reign on the earth.

Postmillennial: This position holds that before Christ returns there will be a worldwide revival. The Church, by the power of the Holy Spirit, will realize the Kingdom of God on earth.

Amillennial: This position holds that the references to a thousand years in Scripture (Revelation 20) are to be taken symbolically, and consequently there will be no literal thousand-year reign of Christ on earth. The "A" means "no" and does not indicate a disbelief in a millennium, but rather a disbelief in a *literal* thousand-year earthly Kingdom. Christ reigns in the Church—in the hearts of believers.

Light on the Text

2:2 "Saying that the day of the Lord has already come." Apparently there was a forged letter saying that the Day of the Lord had come already. Paul tells them that they ought not to be alarmed because the day will not come until the man of lawlessness has come.

"Our being gathered to him." This is the event usually called the rapture of the saints. It is also mentioned by Paul in I Thessalonians 4:15-17 (see Mt. 24:31 also). An ongoing theological discussion is whether or not the Church will be taken out of the world before, or after, the time of tribulation (see Rev. 6—18).

2:3 "For that day will not come until the rebellion occurs and the man of lawlessness is revealed." In some manuscripts this man is called "the man of sin." The difference is not significant, for sin is lawlessness.

To protect them against the danger of deception, Paul introduced two features that must precede the Day of the Lord. "Rebellion" translates the Greek word *apostasia,* from which we get "apostasy." Ordinarily, in the religious realm, apostasy refers to a defiant departure from the living God (see Heb. 6:6; 10:39).

Along with the "rebellion" comes the representative of lawlessness. This person is usually equated with the Antichrist.

"Man doomed to destruction." Paul has no doubt of the ultimate result of this conflict. One could understand the expression "man of lawlessness" as a man characterized by lawlessness. Here the same person is described as the man already condemned to destruction.

2:4, 5 "He opposes and exalts himself over everything that is called God." Verse 4 supplies the chief description of the man of lawlessness. He stations himself both against ("opposes") and above ("exalts himself over") everything that is worshiped. This language reflects Daniel 7:25; 8:9, 10; and 11:36, 37.

"Even sets himself up in God's temple." He is depicted by Paul as taking his seat in the Temple of God. Such action might seem utterly mad to us who have been raised to fear the Lord, but during the time between the Old and New Testaments, a ruler of Syria, Antiochus Epiphanes, had set up an altar in the Jerusalem Temple on which he sacrificed a pig. His abuses led to the Maccabean revolt. Later, the Roman Emperor Gaius (Caligula) attempted to set up a statue of himself in the Temple in A.D. 40. Many commentators feel that these events prefigure the coming of the Antichrist.

"Proclaiming himself to be God." The man of sin commits the ultimate blasphemy, claiming to be God.

Who is this man of lawlessness? There have been several interpretations. One is that he is a Roman emperor. This is not unrealistic, considering the way emperors like Nero claimed divinity. Many Protestants in the Reformation period identified the Pope as the man of sin. Unfortunately, this was based on political reasons, not on exegetical evidence. The conclusion we are forced to reach is that there are many antichrists (I Jn. 2:18), consequently many men of lawlessness. The ultimate man of sin will be revealed in the last days.

For Discussion

1. If you had been a member of the Thessalonian church when the rumors were spreading about the Day of the Lord, do you think you would have believed them?

2. How should we respond to announcements that one of the prophecies about the Second Coming has been fulfilled?

3. List some ways Christ and Christianity can be counterfeited or copied.

4. What can we do to defend ourselves against doctrinal deception? Where does godly common sense fit in?

Window on the Word

Many Antichrists

He got a thank-you note from Rosalyn Carter after he dined with her for his help with the presidential campaign. His work was also appreciated by Hubert Humphrey and Walter Mondale. He was made chairman of the Housing Authority by the mayor of San Francisco.

He was a family man. At one point, some 20,000 people were members of his church. He was ordained in a respected Christian denomination of over two million. He was a friend to all races, served on the Human Rights Commission, distributed food and clothing to the needy, helped people find jobs, and provided counseling services. He told discouraged young people that they could be someone and do good.

Who was he? Jim Jones—the same man who led over 900 people to suicide, and who said "he was the actual God who made the heavens and earth" (*Time*, December 4, 1978).

12

Holding Pattern

Truth to Apply: Because the Holy Spirit dwells in me, I have a restraining influence upon evil in the world.

Key Verse: For the secret power of lawlessness is already at work; but the one who now holds it back will continue to do so till he is taken out of the way (II Thesslonians 2:7).

"What difference do we Christians make, Pastor?" asked Fred. "I mean, look at the world. Look at our planet! There is so much going on that is just terrible. You remember Judy, who was baptized just a couple of months ago? She's now talking about leaving her husband and kids. And what about world hunger, the arms race, and now AIDS! I'm so discouraged I don't know what to do! What's the point? We can't even begin to make a difference."

"Well, Fred . . ."

You be the pastor. How do you answer Fred?

Background/Overview: *II Thessalonians 2:6-15*

Paul continues his discussion of the last days by reminding them that the man of lawlessness is being held back by some person or principle they know. Even while evil is at work, it is being hindered. When the man of lawlessness is revealed, Jesus will destroy him with His breath. Paul goes on to describe the man of lawlessness. He will come with false miracles, deceiving the lost. Finally, Paul tells them to be thankful for their election and sanctification through faith. They should stand firm. He prays that they will be encouraged.

Who is the one who restrains? There have been a number of suggestions. For example: Paul's own missionary work, the Jewish state, the Roman government (which permitted the missionary work to continue uninterrupted by local clashes), Christian believers, the Holy Spirit. At the end of this lesson we will have a better idea of who or what the restrainer is.

Light on the Text

2:6 "You know what is holding him back." In last week's lesson we looked at some of the identifying features of the man of lawlessness. He is an opponent of true religion, and a claimant of deity. This man of sin was being restrained by a principle that is "holding him back." The word in vs. 6 for the restrainer is a neuter in Greek (a thing), but "the one who now holds it back" is masculine in Greek, indicating a person (vs. 7). This adds to the problem of interpretation.

All interpretations of this restraining principle/person must meet this standard: in some way the restraint must involve *both* a force, and a person behind the force. Below are listed the pros and cons of four popular views attempting to identify the restrainer.

1) About 200 A.D., Tertullian held that the restraining principle was the Roman Empire. The government enforced order, preventing lawlessness. The Roman

Empire was personified in the line of its emperors. In favor of this view is the fact that, before Paul wrote the Thessalonians, the magistrates at Philippi (Acts 16:20) and the city officials at Thessalonica (Acts 17:6) had protected him from lawlessness. Against this view some would argue that the Roman Empire passed off the scene without the man of sin appearing, for he is said to be conquered at Christ's Second Coming (II Thess. 2:8).

2) Interpreters like Leon Morris have broadened the first view to the principle of government in general, wherever it is embodied in a personal governor. In Romans 13 Paul speaks favorably of the protective power of government. In objection to this view, one might ask: Is human government powerful enough to hold back the man of sin, who is inspired by Satan?

3) A third view is that the Holy Spirit (living within believers) is the force and figure holding back the man of sin's appearance. In favor of this view is the fact that the Spirit (a grammatical neuter in Greek) is a Person (and so qualifies for the masculine pronoun of vs. 7). The Spirit, it is argued, is strong enough to hold back Satan's henchman until the Spirit (through a pretribulation rapture of the Church?) is taken out of the way (vs. 7). One problem with this view is: Why should all this be significant to the Church if it won't even be on earth at that future time?

4) Another view points to the Gospel as the restraining force. It must be preached throughout the world prior to the end (Mt. 24:14; Mk. 13:10). This powerful force is personified in the personal involvement of preachers or Christian witnesses. But will the Gospel be taken out of the way when the man of sin is revealed?

Are you sufficiently stumped? This is certainly one of the toughest passages in the New Testament. Perhaps your church, pastor, or denomination subscribes to a particular position on this issue. You may need to check with your pastor for help in handling this difficult section of Scripture.

One thing that does come through clearly in all of this is the rule of God. He is sovereign, and in control. Evil cannot run rampant even in its strongest embodiment without the permission of God. The man of lawlessness will not be revealed until the time is right. At present, he is being restrained according to God's will.

2:7 "The secret power of lawlessness is already at work." "Secret" here is the word often translated "mystery." It has nothing to do with Agatha Christie novels. It means "hidden," and often carries the added notion of "impossible to discover without revelation." Paul is probably indicating that there is a principle of great wickedness in the world. This malevolent force or person is perhaps a new idea for pagans, who viewed the gods as more or less human.

"Till he is taken out of the way." This probably refers to the restrainer of the previous verses. Clearly this person is someone closely connected to God's plan for extending the Good News to all the world. If it is the Holy Spirit, the words "taken out of the way" would mean something like "My Spirit will not contend with man forever" (Gen. 6:3).

2:8 "The lawless one will be revealed." This is the third time Paul tells the believers that the lawless one will be revealed. He is very emphatic on that point. One of the events of the last days will be the revelation of this supremely wicked man who will appear, at first, to be very good.

"The Lord Jesus will overthrow." "Lord" has its full force here. At this point God will step in decisively.

"With the breath of his mouth." It will not be an even contest. Jesus needs only his breath. His word shall slay him, as in Luther's great hymn.

"Destroy by the splendor of his coming." In John Milton's *Paradise Lost,* the poet describes the first rebellion of Satan and those angels who followed him. They are driven out of Heaven by Christ's presence.

2:9 "In accordance with the work of Satan." Christ's coming, Paul states in II Thessalonians 2:8, will be with striking splendor. This contrasts with the false splendor of the miracles (2:9) of the man of sin. II Thessalonians 2:9 uses the three chief words for the vocabulary of miracles (compare "miracles, wonders and signs" in Acts 2:22).

These three words have slightly different flavorings, each highlighting some aspect of miracles.

The Greek word for "power" is the word from which we also derive the English word "dynamite." Dynamite is obviously something containing tremendous power. Hence, this Greek word spotlights the awesome nature of supernatural power resident in a miracle.

The word "signs" focuses on the purpose or significance of a miracle. One is to ask, "Why is this happening?" For someone to get all wrapped up in miracles in themselves—without seeking their significance—is like a cross-country driver parking at a highway sign and proceeding to unpack his suitcases, rather than to drive on to the destination.

"Wonders" highlights the spectacular element.

2:10 "They perish because they refused to love the truth and so be saved." These deceptive, diabolical demonstrations strike a responsive chord in them that perish (II Thess. 2:10). Since they did not love the truth (the expression is found only here in the Greek New Testament), they preferred to believe a lie (2:11). Compare this with the expression found in Romans 1:25 where humanity has changed the truth of God into a lie.

2:11 "Powerful delusion." As a result, just as Romans 1 indicates that "God gave them up," even so II Thessalonians 2 says that "God sends them a powerful delusion." Beware of tampering with the truth of God!

2:12 "Delighted in wickedness." We have in view people who are enemies of God, who love evil rather than good, and who will do all in their power to hinder the work of God.

2:13 "From the beginning God chose you." There are several theological terms in these last verses of chapter two. The first theological term, "chosen," recalls the privileges Israel had possessed in the Old Testament (I Pet. 2:9).

"To be saved." Salvation (2:13) is the operative word, portraying the Christian's rescue from sin.

"Through the sanctifying work of the Spirit." The two means of this rescue are through sanctification of the Spirit and belief of the truth (2:13). The Greek word for sanctification is related to the nouns "holiness" and "saints" and to the adjective "holy." The Holy Spirit can make our spirits holy. This is the operation designated "sanctification."

"Through belief in the truth." Truth brings freedom. Those who know and believe the truth are free. But notice that belief is a matter of one's will, not one's head.

2:14, 15 "The glory of our Lord Jesus Christ." The goal of all the theological truth of verse 13 is the obtaining of the glory of our Lord Jesus Christ.

"Hold to the teachings." If belief in the truth is indispensable, then it is imperative to hold to the teachings. Before the New Testament was gathered in a written body, these apostolic "traditions" were crucial.

For Discussion

1. What is your opinion of the several views identifying the restrainer in II Thessalonians 2:6, 7?

2. What is the main characteristic of the man of lawlessness that you see working in your world?

3. How can we fight deceit? What does Paul suggest to the Thessalonian believers?

Window on the Word

Possible Interruption

G. Campbell Morgan once said, "I never begin my work in the morning without thinking that perhaps He may interrupt my work and begin His own. I am not looking for death. I am looking for Him."

13

The Christian and Work

Truth to Apply: If I am able, I should support myself by honest work and not exploit the labor of others.

Key Verse: If a man will not work, he shall not eat (II Thessalonians 3:10).

What does work do for the worker? It gives a sense of worth and identity. It provides reward in the form of money, resulting in power. Everyone should be allowed to share these benefits. Yet powerful groups will sometimes attempt to keep competition down by encouraging minority groups to stay out of the job market.

The Christian has to be concerned with any area of society in which injustice exists. It is scarcely a Christian attitude to force a minority into a position of having no work and then attack that minority on grounds of laziness! Let us be sure we know the facts before we criticize.

What is the employment situation in your community? Does everyone really have a fair chance to work?

Background/Overview: *II Thessalonians 3:1-8*

Paul asks for prayer that the message of the Lord may be spread and honored, and that they may be delivered from wicked men. He warns them to avoid the idle person who will not work. Such people should be avoided in order to shame them into correct behavior. Then Paul pronounces a benediction, and asks them to observe his handwriting as proof of his authorship.

The authority of Paul's apostleship is conspicuous in this third chapter. But in spite of the military language Paul uses, his emphasis is on love and his desire for the advancement of the Kingdom of God.

The Thessalonians had seen love manifested in Paul's own behavior. So that he could be an example to those he sought to lead, he had not demanded what he felt was his right. He labored in love. It was to such labor that he called the Thessalonians.

Light on the Text

3:1-5 "Pray for us." By asking the believers at Thessalonica to pray, Paul is inviting them to join him in the work of spreading the Gospel. If the Word of God is to "spread rapidly" (the Greek word means "to run"), this requires faithful preaching and fervent prayer, both of which mean hard work. When a church thinks of seeking support for missions, generally it thinks in terms of finances. But Paul does not ask for money. He knows the real work of the kingdom depends not merely on money but also on prayer. Therefore, he urges the Thessalonians to labor together with him in intercession.

"That we may be delivered from wicked and evil men." Paul needs prayer not only so that the Word of God will prosper, but also so that God will rescue him from his enemies. The Bible never says the work of God will go forward without opposition. Some will believe the Gospel, but many "wicked" and "evil men" will resist it.

In this case, since he is writing from Corinth, Paul may be referring to the Jews in the synagogue there who troubled him. Or he may be referring to all people who choose not to respond to the Gospel positively. As William Barclay says, "Faith's appeal is not selective; it goes out to every man, but the heart of man can refuse its response." Whenever someone rejects the Gospel, that person becomes automatically a part of the opposition (see Mt. 12:30).

The Greek word translated "wicked" literally means "out of place." When any person is "out of place" with the will of God, that person becomes an obstacle to the free course of the Gospel.

"For not everyone has faith. But the Lord is faithful." Paul plays on the words "faith" and "faithful." Not all people accept the faith, but God is faithful to strengthen those who do believe, and to shield them from evil (or the Evil One). Not only that, He will lead them into loving Him and into patient persistence. The two concerns in these verses are the need to work for the salvation of others (vss. 1, 2) and the need to work out one's own salvation (vss. 3-5).

3:6 "Keep away from every brother who is idle" does not mean to reject utterly. Instead, it means to have no intimate fellowship with. In his first letter to the Thessalonians, Paul exhorted the people to "Make it your ambition to lead a quiet life, to mind your own business and to work with your hands, just as we told you" (I Thess. 4:11). Belief in the Lord's early return must have caused some of the Thessalonians to quit working for their livelihood.

3:8 "Nor did we eat anyone's food without paying for it." While in Thessalonica, Paul had worked hard. He labored day and night, supporting himself so he did not have to live off any of the Thessalonians. Paul has little to say in any of his letters about his own financial needs. When he raised money, it was for the support of the church in Jerusalem, which was beset by difficult times. Whatever needs he may have had, he learned to live with them. He wrote, "I know what it is to be in need, and I know what it is to have plenty. I have learned the secret of being content in any and every situation, whether well fed or hungry, whether living in plenty or in want" (Phil. 4:12).

Yet a few verses later he gratefully acknowledged the Philippians' generosity while he was preaching in Thessalonica: "Moreover, as you Philippians know, in the early days of your acquaintance with the gospel, when I set out from Macedonia, not one church shared with me in the matter of giving and receiving, except you only; for even when I was in Thessalonica, you sent me aid again and again when I was in need" (Phil. 4:15, 16).

The Thessalonians may have become aware of the support sent by the church at Philippi and joined with them in sending financial support to Paul after he left their city. If so, that was a beautiful response to Paul's request for prayer: they prayed and they gave. Isn't this what usually happens when people begin to pray?

3:10-18 In these verses, Paul is speaking of the responsibility for doing those things necessary to maintain life. The principle he states in verse 10 is referred to as the golden rule of work: "If a man will not work, he shall not eat." The maxim is brief and pointed, and reflects the Jewish attitude toward work. Expressed in this simple rule is the basic conviction that work is not only necessary, and therefore required, but good, and therefore sanctified. Those who believe that Jesus is the Christ demonstrate that confidence by their example of working quietly and providing for themselves sufficiently.

Paul directs the believers to shame those who fail to follow his commands by breaking fellowship with them. This punishment may seem strong to us, but it shows the seriousness with which Paul viewed the matter of responsible employment. Idleness and laziness are contradictions of God's will for Christian living.

Paul ends this passage with a benediction of peace. The Hebrew word for peace, *shalom,* basically means "wholeness" or "completeness." As Leon Morris puts it, peace is a "comprehensive term for the prosperity of the whole man." Wholeness involves not only the spiritual life, but the physical as well.

Paul's teaching about diligent labor was backed by his example. As an apostle, he had the authority to be supported financially by those to whom he preached, by those he taught (I Cor. 9:3-14). But he didn't exercise this right. Rather than depending on anyone for his support, he toiled night and day as an example of industriousness. (Paul worked as a tentmaker, Acts 18:3; I Thess. 2:9.)

3:11 Evidently, someone had succeeded in convincing the Christians at Thessalonica, by forging a letter in Paul's name, that the Day of the Lord had come (II Thess. 2:2). When the people heard this word, many of them felt there was no need to continue working, since their efforts would all be for naught when Jesus returned from Heaven.

Those who quit working began to get involved in the business of others. Some were finding it necessary to sponge off others because they no longer were providing for themselves. Perhaps a number had become so "spiritual" that they thought involvement in the workaday world was beneath their dignity. Such spurious spirituality has been the bane of Christianity throughout history. It still can be found in some people today.

3:13 "Never tire of doing what is right." Paul encourages the believers to persevere because he knows that endurance in right doing is difficult, but necessary.

3:14, 15 To "warn," or admonish, is to speak with gravity to a person regarding the error in his or her life. This social pressure was designed to encourage someone to do what was right. It was the kind of discipline that should exist in a family. If family members do something wrong, they should have to bare the responsibility of their own actions. But after the discipline, life should go on.

3:16 Paul prayed for all the members of the Thessalonian church; even for the idlers! Believers should ask themselves: Do I intercede for all God's children, the strong and the weak, the dedicated and the wayward?

For Discussion

1. If you had been a member of the congregation at Thessalonica, what would you have done when you heard the apostolic command to shun the loafers? Would it have been difficult for you to obey this directive? How does this command apply to us today?

2. Discuss the Biblical teaching regarding work. These verses will help you discover God's attitude toward work: Gen. 2:15; 23:12; Prov. 6:6; 10:5; 12:11; 13:11; 14:23; 20:13; 22:20; Rom. 12:11; Eph. 4:28; 6:5-8; I Tim. 5:8.

3. Should Christians get welfare aid from the state?

Window on the Word

Thank God for Work?

Almost everyone has heard the expression, "Thank God it's Friday!" Not many of us have ever heard someone say, "Thank God it's Monday!" Work does not generate that response in most of us.

Charles Kingsley, a nineteenth-century author, once wrote in a letter quite a different opinion: "Thank God every morning when you get up that you have something to do that day which must be done, whether you like it or not. Being forced to work, and forced to do your best, will breed in you temperance and self-control, diligence and strength of will, cheerfulness and content, and a hundred virtues which the idle never know."

How different life would be if we learned to begin the day with this prayer: "Thank God for work!"

Leader Helps and Lesson Plan

General Guidelines for Group Study

*Open and close each session with prayer.

*Since the lesson texts are not printed in the book, group members should have their Bibles with them for each study session.

*As the leader, prepare yourself for each session through personal study (during the week) of the Bible text and lesson. On notepaper, jot down any points of interest or concern as you study. Jot down your thoughts about how God is speaking to you through the text, and how He might want to speak to the entire group. Look up cross-reference passages (as they are referred to in the lessons), and try to find answers to questions that come to your mind. Also, recall stories from your own life experience that could be shared with the group to illustrate points in the lesson.

*Try to get participation from everyone. Get to know the more quiet members through informal conversation before and after the sessions. Then, during the study, watch for nonverbal signs (a change in expression or posture) that they would like to respond. Call on them. Say: "What are your thoughts on this, Sue?"

*Don't be afraid of silence. Adults need their own space. Often a long period of silence after a question means the group has been challenged to do some real thinking—hard work that can't be rushed!

*Acknowledge each contribution. No question is a dumb question. Every comment, no matter how "wrong," comes from a worthy person, who needs to be affirmed as valuable to the group. Find ways of tactfully accepting the speaker while guiding the discussion back on track: "Thank you for that comment, John; now what do some of the others think?" or, "I see your point, but are you aware of . . . ?"

When redirecting the discussion, however, be sensitive to the fact that sometimes the topic of the moment *should be* the "sidetrack" because it hits a felt need of the participants.

*Encourage *well-rounded* Christian growth. Christians are called to grow in knowledge of the Word, but they are also challenged to grow in love and wisdom. This means that they must constantly develop in their ability to wisely apply the Bible knowledge to their experience.

Lesson Plan

The following four-step lesson plan can be used effectively for each chapter, varying the different suggested approaches from lesson to lesson.

STEP 1: *Focus on Life Need*

The opening section of each lesson is an anecdote, quote, or other device designed to stimulate sharing on how the topic relates to practical daily living. There are many ways to do this. For example, you might list on the chalkboard the group's answers to: "How have you found this theme relevant to your daily life?" "What are your past successes, or failures, in this area?" "What is your present level of struggle or victory with this?" "Share a story from your own experience relating to this topic."

Sharing questions are designed to be open-ended and allow people to talk about themselves. The questions allow for sharing about past experiences, feelings, hopes and dreams, fears and anxieties, faith, daily life, likes and dislikes, sorrows and joys. Self-disclosure results in group members' coming to know each other at a more intimate level. This kind of personal sharing is necessary to experience deep affirmation and love.

However you do it, the point is to get group members to share *where they are now* in relation to the Biblical topic. As you seek to get the group involved, remember the following characteristics of good sharing questions:[1]

1. Good sharing questions encourage risk without forcing participants to go beyond their willingness to respond.

2. Good sharing questions begin with low risk and build toward higher risk. (It is often good, for instance, to ask a history question to start, then build to present situations in people's lives.)

3. Sharing questions should not require people to confess their sins or to share only negative things about themselves.

4. Questions should be able to be answered by every member of the group.

5. The questions should help the group members to know one another better and learn to love and understand each other more.

6. The questions should allow for enough diversity in response so each member does not wind up saying the same thing.

7. They should ask for sharing of self, not for sharing of opinions.

STEP 2: *Focus on Bible Learning*

Use the "Light on the Text" section for this part of the lesson plan. Again, there are a number of ways to get group members involved, but the emphasis here is more on learning Bible content than on applying it. Below are some suggestions on how to proceed. The methods could be varied from week to week.

*Lecture on important points in the Bible passage (from your personal study notes).

*Assign specific verses in the Bible passage to individuals. Allow five or ten minutes for them to jot down 1) questions, 2) comments, 3) points of concern raised by the text. Then have them share in turn what they have written down.

*Pick important or controversial verses from the passage. In advance, do a personal study to find differences of interpretation among commentators. List and explain these "options" on a blackboard and invite comments concerning the relative merits of each view. Summarize and explain your own view, and challenge other group members to further study.

*Have class members do their own outline of the Bible passage. This is done by giving an original title to each section, chapter, and paragraph, placing each under its appropriate heading according to subject matter. Share the outlines and discuss.

*Make up your own sermons from the Bible passage. Each sermon could include: Title, Theme Sentence, Outline, Illustration, Application, Benediction. Share and discuss.

*View works of art based on the text. Discuss.

*Individually, or as a group, paraphrase the Bible passage in your own words. Share and discuss.

*Have a period of silent meditation upon the Bible passage. Later, share insights.

STEP 3: *Focus on Bible Application*

Most adults prefer group discussion above any other learning method. Use the "For Discussion" section for each lesson to guide a good discussion on the lesson topic and how it relates to felt needs.

Students can benefit from discussion in a number of important ways:[2]

1. Discussion stimulates interest and thinking, and helps students develop the skills of observation, analysis, and hope.

2. Discussion helps students clarify and review what they have learned.

3. Discussion allows students to hear opinions that are more mature and perhaps more Christlike than their own.

4. Discussion stimulates creativity and aids students in applying what they have learned.

5. When students verbalize what they believe and are forced to explain or defend what they say, their convictions are strengthened and their ability to share what they believe with others is increased.

There are many different ways to structure a discussion. All have group interaction as their goal. All provide an opportunity to share in the learning process.

But using different structures can add surprise to a discussion. It can mix people in unique ways. It can allow new people to talk.

Total Class Discussion

In some small classes, all students are able to participate in one effective discussion. This can build a sense of class unity, and it allows everyone to hear the wisdom of peers. But in most groups, total class discussion by itself is unsatisfactory because there is usually time for only a few to contribute.

Buzz Groups

Small groups of three to ten people are assigned any topic for discussion. They quickly select a chairperson and a secretary. The chairperson is responsible for keeping the discussion on track, and the secretary records the group's ideas, reporting the relevant ones to the total class.

Brainstorming

Students, usually in small groups, are presented with a problem and asked to come up with as many different solutions as possible. Participants should withhold judgment until all suggestions (no matter how creative!) have been offered. After a short break, the group should pick the best contribution from those suggested and refine it. Each brainstorming group will present its solution in a total class discussion.

Forum Discussion

Forum discussion is especially valuable when the subject is difficult and the students would not be able to participate in a meaningful discussion without quite a bit of background. People with special training or experience have insights which would not ordinarily be available to the students. Each forum member should prepare a three- to five-minute speech and be given uninterrupted time in which to present it. Then students should be encouraged to interact with the speakers, either directly or through a forum moderator.

Debate

As students prepare before class for their parts in a debate, they should remember that it is the affirmative side's repsonsibility to prove that the resolve is correct. The negative has to prove that it isn't. Of course, the negative may also want to present an alternative proposal.

There are many ways to structure a debate, but the following pattern is quite effective.

1. First affirmative speech
2. First negative speech
3. Second affirmative speech
4. Second negative speech

(brief break while each side plans its rebuttal)

5. First negative rebuttal
6. First affirmative rebuttal
7. Second negative rebuttal
8. Second affirmative rebuttal.

Floating Panel

Sometimes you have a topic to which almost everyone in the room would have something to contribute, for example: marriage, love, work, getting along with people. For a change of pace, have a floating panel: four or five people, whose names are chosen at random, will become "experts" for several minutes. These people sit in chairs in the front of the room while you and other class members ask them questions. The questions should be experience related. When the panel has been in front for several minutes, enough time for each person to make several comments, draw other names and replace the original members.

Interview As Homework

Ask students to interview someone during the week and present what they learned in the form of short reports the following Sunday.

Interview in Class

Occasionally it is profitable to schedule an in-class interview, perhaps with a visiting missionary or with someone who has unique insights to share with the group. One person can take charge of the entire interview, structuring and asking questions. But whenever possible the entire class should take part. Each student should write a question to ask the guest.

In-Group Interview

Divide the class into groups of three, called triads. Supply all groups with the same question or discussion topic. A in the group interviews B while C listens. Then B interviews C while A listens. Finally C interviews A while B listens. Each interview should take from one to three minutes. When the triads return to the class, each person reports on what was heard rather than said.

Following every class period in which you use discussion, ask yourself these questions to help determine the success of your discussion time:

1. In what ways did this discussion contribute to the group's understanding of today's lesson?
2. If each person was not involved, what can I do next week to correct the situation?
3. In what ways did content play a role in the discussion? (I.e., people were not simply sharing off-the-top-of-their-head opinions.)
4. What follow-up, if any, should be made on the discussion? (For example, if participants showed a lack of knowledge, or misunderstanding in some area of Scripture, you may want to cover this subject soon during the class hour. Or, if they discussed decisions they were making or projects they felt the class should be involved in, follow-up outside the class hour may be necessary.)

STEP 4: *Focus on Life Response*

This step tries to incorporate a bridge from the Bible lesson to actual daily living. It should be a *specific* suggestion as to "how we are going to *do* something about this," either individually, or as a group. Though this is a goal to aim for, it is unlikely that everyone will respond to every lesson. But it is good to have a suggested life response ready for that one or two in the group who may have been moved by *this* lesson to respond *this week* in a tangible way.

Sometimes a whole group will be moved by one particular lesson to do a major project in light of their deepened understanding of, and commitment to, God's will. Such a response would be well worth the weeks of study that may have preceded it.

Examples of life response activities:

1. A whole class, after studying Scriptural principles of evangelism, decides to host an outreach Bible study in a new neighborhood.
2. As a result of studying one of Paul's prayers for the Ephesians, a group member volunteers to start and oversee a church prayer chain for responding to those in need.
3. A group member invites others to join her in memorizing the key verse for the week.
4. Two group members, after studying portions of the Sermon on the Mount, write and perform a song about peacemaking.

Obviously, only you and your group can decide how to respond appropriately to the challenge of living for Christ daily. But the possibilities are endless.

[1]From *Using the Bible in Groups,* by Roberta Hestenes.

[2]The material on discussion methods is adapted from *Creative Teaching Methods,* by Marlene D. LeFever, available from your local Christian bookstore or from David C. Cook Publishing Co., 850 N. Grove Ave., Elgin, IL 60120. Order number: 25254. $14.95. This book contains step-by-step directions for dozens of methods appropriate for use in adult classes.